HOPE
FOR AMERICAN
EVANGELICALS

A MISSIONARY PERSPECTIVE ON

RESTORING OUR BROKEN HOUSE

MATTHEW BENNETT

B&H
PUBLISHING
BRENTWOOD, TENNESSEE

Published by B&H Publishing Group
Brentwood, Tennessee

Dewey Decimal Classification: 261.1
Subject Heading: CHURCH / EVANGELICALISM / UNITED
STATES—RELIGION

Cover design and illustration by Matthew Stevens.

1 2 3 4 5 6 • 27 26 25 24 23

Dedication and Acknowledgments

To Steve and Lynn and Amanda and Kristin for all the ways you made the house at 847 North 6th Street our home

This book is the product of many things and many people.

On one hand, it is the product of my gratitude for things learned and experienced while living with my family in North Africa and the Middle East. I have come to see the world through lenses that have been indelibly shaped by the people we fellowshipped with and the places in which the Lord planted our lives during our years serving as missionaries. I am also grateful for the roots the Lord gave me in my upbringing, my church, and the broader evangelical circles in which I have lived. Those evangelical roots go back to my childhood, and they are also actively keeping me planted today as I remain convinced of the core evangelical commitments to scriptural authority and Christ-centered exclusivity—even amidst all of the contemporary brokenness that evangelicalism seems to be struggling with.

On the other hand, this book is also the direct product of many people who have spoken into it along the way. I want to specifically acknowledge my editors, Taylor Combs and Ashley

Gorman, for help in bringing this idea to reality. Thank you for your efforts, your insight, and your wisdom as you combed through chapters that are now much better due to your feedback and suggestions.

I also want to thank my colleagues at Cedarville University—specifically Josh Bowman, Brandon Smith, Adam Hammett, and Justin Cole—for their willingness to offer feedback on various sections and chapters. In addition, thanks to Cam and Brianna for their insights as those who read early chapters from the perspective of student readers. And thanks also to Ben Doty, Paul Warzecha, Brian Haville, and Kyle Reschke, who read chapters as longtime friends with whom I have tried to cultivate these practices of viewing the world missionally.

Finally, thank you to Emily, my long-suffering and insightful wife. Thank you for slogging through my rough drafts, for pushing back where I needed to hear it, and for encouraging me where things needed to be said more directly. Your wisdom, patience, and encouragement have made this book much better than it would have been otherwise.

Of course, every author bears the responsibility for any errors or oversights in the work that bears his or her name. While I acknowledge that the book is better because of the many eyes that have looked it over, I recognize the mistakes and omissions that yet remain are my fault alone. Still, though, in these brief acknowledgments listed above, I want to give honor and gratitude where they are due. Thank you all for your kind and generous sharing of your time and wisdom.

Contents

Foreword

A great way to see your culture—to really see your world—is to get outside it for a while. When you return home, you'll arrive with fresh eyes. What everyone else takes for granted will stand out. Assumptions and behaviors everyone thinks are "normal" or "just the way it's done" will appear strange and contingent. You'll appreciate some aspects of your past more than ever before, but you'll wonder why certain practices and principles are so pervasive because now you've seen other ways of living, of worshipping, of relating. Without doubt, you'll see areas that could be improved.

This was my experience after living and serving in Eastern Europe for five years in my early twenties. I left the United States with a one-way ticket, immersed myself in another world, did my best to master a new language, to adapt to unfamiliar customs, and serve the church in ways I had never considered before. I cannot begin to quantify the impact that cross-cultural mission work had on me. The personal impact was substantive: it was where I learned to preach, where I married my wife, and where we began our family. The cultural impact was big, too: it changed the way I see the United States, giving me a bigger and more global view of

Christianity while allowing me the opportunity to see contemporary Western culture and the church from the outside in.

I often tell people these days to stay connected to the global church if you want to hold on to orthodoxy . . . and if you want to hold on to your sanity. One of the best ways to maintain sound doctrine and gain perspective on some of our society's most heated debates is to stay in close contact with Christians in other parts of the world. Cultural quirks and theological distinctions will help you discern what's essential and where Christians can "agree to disagree."

Everyone loves that phrase: "in the essentials, unity; in the nonessentials, liberty; in all things, charity." But that only works if you know the difference between essentials and nonessentials. That's why I tell people to stay connected to the church around the world. Nothing puts our squabbles in perspective and aids our discernment of what is most important than reading the Bible alongside our worldwide family of faith. By listening and learning from people in other parts of the world, our eyes can be open to areas of compromise and challenge in our own context that we might be blind to otherwise.

The missionary theologian Lesslie Newbigin spent decades of service in India, and when he returned, he brought new insights—diagnosing ills, pointing to problems, calling out idolatries the church had too often colluded with. He didn't see the United Kingdom as "home base," but as a different mission field, and he longed to see the church have a missionary encounter with the contemporary Western world.

Matthew Bennett has drawn deeply from the wells of Lesslie Newbigin's wisdom. He sees aspects of contemporary Christianity in the West that need to be challenged by a global perspective so we become more biblically faithful and missionally effective. But Matthew is not just a reader of missionary insights; he has spent significant time outside of the United States. He knows the feeling I've often recounted of finding the "culture shock" to be stronger when returning home than when initially arriving on the "mission field." You run into surprises you didn't expect. You see things, too many things—some of them you'd rather stay blind to!

In the end, the church benefits from cross-cultural wisdom. This is why I warmly recommend Matthew Bennett's insights to you. He expresses sharp critique and deep concern, but his humble approach and carefully chosen words indicate a pastoral heart for the good of the church. This is not another voice delivering more heat than light. Bennett acknowledges his own temptations as he wrestles with some of the vices so often accepted in American culture. You may not agree with all of his diagnoses or prescriptions, but you will be better for stretching yourself and listening carefully to a cross-cultural missionary who loves the church.

Be ready to be strengthened, encouraged, and better yet—to see things you may have missed in the church today and then respond with truth and grace to the challenges before us.

—Trevin Wax, vice president of research and resource development at the North American Mission Board, visiting professor at Cedarvillle University, and author of *The Thrill of Orthodoxy*

Chapter 1

Coming Home

A Fresh Look at the Familiar

Perhaps, like me, you've had the experience of returning to a place that was once familiar, only to find it different than you remember. Maybe it was a favorite vacation spot, a cabin in the woods, or an old schoolyard. Despite having fond memories connected to that space, upon returning to it you are likely to notice things your memory or your proximity hadn't previously allowed you to see. The defects you once overlooked in their familiarity now seem to stand out after the passing of time.

I encountered this phenomenon when my family sold the house I grew up in. When I returned to help my mom and sisters get the place ready for sale, it had been six years since I had lived there. During that time we had lost my father unexpectedly, so the place felt different. Still, the house was intimately familiar, and the task of preparing it for sale was full of nostalgia, heartache, laughter, and tears as my mom, sisters, and I reminisced our way through the cleaning, packing, and staging. This place had provided the environment in which I was nurtured, had fed my vision of what family was supposed to be, and had been in many ways the backdrop for my adolescent formation. I loved this house because of the way my family had made it my home.

However, at the same time as the space was familiar, I also saw it with new eyes. Since the house needed to be presentable to someone who didn't have twenty years of the appreciation that familiarity can create, it needed to be inspected by a detached observer. As I tried to view the house from a potential buyer's perspective, I noticed that the floorboards of the entryway were saggier than I remembered. Likewise, I realized that the musty smell of the three-season porch that reminded me of summer nights and conversations with Dad would not convey the same fond memories to a visitor. The bedrooms that had hosted my sisters and me through our formative years were much smaller than I recalled. The paint colors we had chosen years before were long out of style. The way the cabinet doors stuck when the humidity crept in through open windows, though familiar to my muscle memory, stood out differently as I walked the well-trodden linoleum floors of the kitchen. And the backyard—most of which had been cemented over as a dedicated basketball court—suddenly seemed as though it had sacrificed its potential for manicured beauty to accommodate my unlikely sports dreams.

While this place functioned as an inviting and beloved house that had served my family and me well, the fondness I had for my childhood home had perhaps clouded my apprehension of some of its infelicities.

In reality, the space had not actually changed much since I had been gone. The rooms had not gotten smaller. The bold colors of the walls were not new. The yard had not radically deteriorated. But as I returned home during that season with a desire to help make the space presentable for someone else to consider, I saw the same house through new eyes.

The thing I realized along the way was that I do not remember a time our cabinet doors did not stick. But I also do not remember ever thinking twice about it. We could have taken the doors off their hinges, sanded down the edges, stained them more precisely, and rehung them more carefully. But the working solution was much easier. And it was something to which we had accommodated our habits: you just had to pull harder. It wasn't a fix. It didn't address the problem. But it was familiar, it was engrained, and it was what we did. We were used to it being that way, and there was no compelling reason to change. That is, there was no reason to change until we began to think of the space as it would appear to an outsider.

Coming Home to the American Church

A few years ago, my family and I experienced another kind of homecoming in which we encountered a similar phenomenon. We found ourselves returning not just to a home, but to a home country. Having lived in North Africa and the Middle East for most of seven years, we found ourselves transitioning back to life in the culture in which we were raised. I was grateful to take a job teaching missions and theology at an evangelical university here in the familiar cornfields of the Midwest.

In addition to teaching at the university, we have found a welcoming community of believers at a local Baptist church within walking distance from our home. This church is wonderfully similar to the churches my wife and I grew up in. In addition to being members of the church, I have also recently been entrusted with the task of serving as an elder—a role that continually overwhelms me with the magnitude of its responsibility. In both settings I am being challenged and encouraged by my colleagues, coworkers, and church family. In both settings I find myself experiencing a sort of homecoming after living as a religious minority in a very different cultural environment.

> A missionary perspective is vital to considering how today's American evangelical house might better display the gospel.

Simply stated, I love this evangelical university, and I love my evangelical church.

Yet as we have recently returned to ministry spaces similar to those we grew up in, my wife and I have noticed the mission field has changed some of our outlook. What I want to argue in this book comes from some of our experience of looking around the evangelical house through these missionary lenses. I believe that a missionary perspective is vital to considering how today's American evangelical house might better display the gospel and serve as the pillar and buttress of the truth that Paul says it is intended to be.

There are several missionary skills and perspectives that will prove helpful in this task. During our missionary training, we were challenged to look at the broader world around us and our global neighbors differently than we had been doing. We needed to study our new neighbors, their culture, and their language so we could make sure that when we shared the gospel we would be understood. This task is called contextualization. But what we have come to realize is that contextualization is just as important at home.

Additionally, we needed to learn how to live as foreigners in a country where we were not natural-born citizens. Contrary to our assumptions of our American upbringing, we could not expect the government to advocate for or even protect our freedoms. We were minorities whose presence within the borders of a foreign country was always tenuous. Such a perspective can help us recognize ways we have grown accustomed to expecting our earthly citizenship to fill the role of our heavenly citizenship.

And, perhaps more than any other influence on our view of ministry and the church, we were humbled and convicted as we watched our brothers and sisters in Christ faithfully live out the gospel in the midst of the persecution and daily hardships that resulted from their faith. The way they persistently and joyfully clung to Christ in the midst of those who sought to take everything else away from them has indelibly marked my own understanding of the preciousness of the gospel.

As a result of our training and experience as missionaries, we have been changed in significant ways. As any person living in a sin-sick world who still battles their flesh, we have our own blind spots and persistent failures. But having returned and considered some of the most pressing issues the American church is facing, I am convinced the missionary lenses we were trained to look through can help Christians see some of the confusing and frustrating elements of Western culture today with a little more clarity.

Lesslie Newbigin: A Missionary's Homecoming

I am certainly not the first returning missionary to recognize the benefits of looking at the Western church with missionary lenses. In fact, I hope throughout this book to introduce you to someone who did this long before me—Lesslie Newbigin.

Newbigin was a twentieth-century missiologist whose missionary experience made him a better minister at home. For those unfamiliar with Newbigin, a brief introduction of his life, ministry, and writings will provide a helpful context before we begin.

Born and raised in England at the beginning of the twentieth century, Newbigin enjoyed a happy, well-cared-for upbringing. During his time as a university student at Queens College, Newbigin was converted to Christ and became enamored with the church. This newfound gospel life and the church community he joined set the trajectory for his ministry. In 1936, seeking to announce this good news to the ends of the earth, Lesslie and his new bride, Helen, departed from Liverpool, having been appointed as missionaries with the Foreign Mission Committee of the Church of Scotland.[1] Their destination was Madras, India.

---

1. Paul Weston, ed., *Lesslie Newbigin: Missionary Theologian* (Grand Rapids: Eerdmans, 2006), 5.

The Newbigins served as missionaries in India for thirty-eight years, during which time Lesslie was involved in a wide variety of activities. He engaged in personal evangelism and disciple-making, while also being appointed to positions of leadership in various ministerial communities.[2] Beyond the things that Newbigin was involved in leading, however, he was also cultivating what one of his students referred to as a "missional ecclesiology."[3] In other words, through his writings and ministry, Newbigin was setting out a vision of local churches as the key to Christian mission in the world.

In 1974, Lesslie and Helen determined it was time to leave India. They embarked on a two-month-long overland journey from Madras, India, to Birmingham, England, where Lesslie was to serve for five years as a lecturer at Selly Oak Colleges.[4] This retirement suited Newbigin, but when he became aware of a struggling church on the verge of having to close its doors, the seventy-two-year-old man stepped in to serve as the pastor of Mary Hill United Reformed Church in inner-city Birmingham. The struggling church was multi-cultural, primarily composed of Indian and Caribbean immigrants. Being located directly across the street from Winson Green prison and adjacent to an asylum and a foundry, it was often unflatteringly referred to as "Merry

2. Geoffrey Wainwright, *Lesslie Newbigin: A Theological Life* (Eugene, OR: Wipf & Stock, 2000), 9.

3. See the helpful synthesis that appears to coin this term as a summation of Newbigin's thought and contribution compiled by Michael Goheen, *The Church and Its Vocation: Lesslie Newbigin's Missionary Ecclesiology* (Grand Rapids: Baker, 2018).

4. Westin, *Lesslie Newbigin: Missionary Theologian*, 11–12.

Hell."[5] Despite the inauspicious beginnings of this late-in-life endeavor, it was in these home-country ecclesial environs that Newbigin's training and experience as a missionary-theologian were put to some of their most fruitful use.

Even while he had been living in a foreign context, Newbigin's concerns for his home culture never waned. He was haunted by a question raised by T. B. Simatupang, "Can the West be [re] converted?"[6] And in his ministry to the parishioners at Mary Hill and the surrounding English context, his cross-cultural tools proved imminently helpful in the work of applying the whole gospel to the whole of life.[7]

The reason I bring Lesslie Newbigin's story to the fore—even in such a brief treatment—is to chart the course for where this book intends to go. Having learned to don missionary lenses for viewing the world of competing idols around him in India, Newbigin was postured well to return home and to recognize places where idols had infiltrated his home country as well. Even though the idols he discovered in England in the latter part of the twentieth century were different than those adorning the shrines and homes of his neighbors in Madras, he had learned to see with missionary eyes where worship was being directed away from the Creator and to the created.

---

5. Wainwright, *Lesslie Newbigin: A Theological Life*, 14.

6. Wainwright, *Lesslie Newbigin: A Theological Life*, 14.

7. While many of Newbigin's writings are available through book sellers, it is an incredible convenience of modernity to note there is an extensive online database that hosts many resources from Newbigin's writings to be accessed at https://newbiginresources.org.

In response to the question, "Can the West be reconverted?," Newbigin offered an optimistic answer. But his optimism did not preclude him from offering significant criticism. As I have worked my way back through Newbigin's writings, I have consistently found him interpreting for me some of my own inarticulate discomfort upon coming home.

From the outset it is good to note that, like any other human guide, there are aspects of Newbigin's approach that are open to critique. For instance, I wish he were clearer in his writing to affirm that the gospel is the exclusive means of salvation. Likewise, while he consistently pointed to the supreme authority of the Scriptures, he did not affirm biblical inerrancy. But despite these shortcomings, as we progress through this book, I hope to lean into some of Newbigin's many insights to provide a jumping-off point for our inspection of our own situation as American evangelicals.

The American Evangelical House

As we work through these pages, I want us to walk around the American evangelical house together with fresh eyes. We will attempt to bring out the beauty of the church for those who don't have the proximity or history to overlook its blemishes. Along the way, we will encounter some sticky cabinets that need attention. At times, we may even need to get down under the house and reinforce the foundation. But it is worth the effort of inspection to make sure this household of God displays for the coming generations the wonderful blessings of community from which we have benefitted.

Now, there is one major difference between the analogy of the pre-sale inspection of my childhood home and what we intend to do in this inspection of the evangelical church. The difference is my family was moving out of my childhood home so that someone else could move in. My desire is to encourage us to inspect the evangelical house with an eye to inviting others in and with the intention of staying ourselves.

For anyone who has paid attention to the state of American evangelicalism over the past two decades or so, it should come as no surprise that there are elements of our practice needing inspection. Well-known ministers of the gospel have been discovered to be embroiled in any number of illicit and egregious sin patterns. Sexual and emotional abuses have been covered up for years in order to protect the ministry brand or the denominational reputation. Lies, adultery, scandal, greed, power-grabbing, and self-aggrandizement have been featured all-too-often in the evangelical news cycle. Racial tensions have not merely been a problem in American streets, but at times in American sanctuaries. And we have seen the aftermath of church leaders who have been wooed by celebrity and have shipwrecked their ministry as they have neglected the sheep in pursuit of the platform.

Some might be tempted to ask the question, "Can American Evangelicalism be reconverted?"

Like Newbigin, I am optimistic that the evangelical house can yet be restored into a beautiful home. But also like Newbigin, I believe that a missionary's perspective is necessary to reveal some significant criticisms that many American evangelical churches would do well to consider.

Like coming back to a childhood home with new eyes, the following chapters will inspect the various rooms of our evangelical house. We will examine *our neighborhood* (the changing cultural context of American evangelicalism); the *dining room* (where we consider racial tensions and multicultural ministry); the *living room* (where we see the hypocrisy between what we say and how we live); the *bedroom* (where we discover that we have not fully rejected the sexual idolatry of the world); our *yard* (where we consider whether we're more focused on looking presentable or using our space purposefully); and our *address* (where we think about our true citizenship).

> **I am optimistic that the evangelical house can yet be restored into a beautiful home.**

Since Newbigin has paved the way for this type of exploration, we will consider his insights in each room. However, since Newbigin's writings focused on issues pertinent to the late twentieth century, some of the immediate concerns we are encountering even just a few decades after his passing need to be updated and made more contemporary. As we tour the house with Newbigin as our guide, I hope you will be convinced that a missionary approach is essential as we evangelicals respond to the world around us—and even the world within our churches—with grace, love, and a desire to support and display the beauty of the gospel of Jesus Christ in a broken world.

A Word of Recognition

With Newbigin, I am convinced the church is God's primary vehicle for his mission in the world. Thus, I am praying as I work though this book that any critique I offer—both through specific suggestions and the tone used to offer them—would convey my deep love for and abiding commitment to the evangelical church. As such, I write from the posture of one who is seeking first and foremost to invite the Holy Spirit to bring conviction to the ways I have accommodated the gospel to my preferences, as one who longs to live out this Christian life in the context of the covenant community of my church, and as one who is immovably committed to the idea that God does not just have a mission for the church, but that he has the church for his mission.[8]

With that said, I should acknowledge at the outset that this is both an insider-critique and a self-critique. I love the church and am committed to it. I love the freedoms God has—during this time in world history—afforded to American churches and I am a beneficiary thereof. I am also very aware that many of these critiques and the changes they call for must begin with myself—I am culpable for some of the very failures and missteps I will be investigating. I have benefitted from the perspective of many in my current church who have shown me aspects of our context to which I am oblivious as a newcomer. I therefore write and observe humbly and with a desire that the Spirit use this project to prompt

---

8. Christopher J. H. Wright, *The Mission of God* (Downers Grove, IL: IVP Academic, 2006), 62.

changes in me as the author even while suggesting changes in you, the reader.

I also recognize that any time someone speaks a critical word against the so-called "evangelical" church, there is a good chance no church actually embodies the characterization that follows. I recognize that it is a myth to think there is some monolithic thing called American Evangelicalism. Each individual church will wrestle differently with various aspects of this investigation. In some areas, your church may be well developed, while in others, you may find a need for significant attention.

> **It is a myth to think there is some monolithic thing called American Evangelicalism.**

Furthermore, in this book I am not interested in debating the utility of the word "evangelical" or deciding definitively who is in and who is out.[9] For the sake of simple clarity, I use "evangelical" according to the broadly agreed upon categories offered by David Bebbington: those who are committed to (1) biblical centrality, (2) Christ's atonement on the cross, (3) the necessity of individual conversion, and (4) a gospel-driven life of active sanctification and outreach.[10] If this describes you

---

9. A helpful treatment for those interested in some of the contemporary discussions around this issue can be found in Thomas Kidd, *Who Is an Evangelical?* (New Haven, CT: Yale University Press, 2020).

10. Often referred to as the Bebbington Quadrilateral, these four points can be found in David Bebbington, *Evangelicalism in Modern Britain* (New York: Routledge, 1988), 2–3.

or your church, then I would love for you to join me in this self-inspection.

Finally, I have a request to make of you as you read through these pages: Would you read and hear me as a brother in Christ? I recognize there may be times when my suggestions might be ill-suited to your situation. I also recognize you possess a lot more expertise about your particular congregation, community, and context than I do. I do not want to write presumptuously as though I knew what you have been doing wrong and were ready and equipped to prescribe the remedy. Rather, my desire is to encourage you to step back with me, consider your context, community, and congregation as a missionary would, and then assess what aspects of your ministry might benefit from this approach. My intent is to lend you my lenses as one who has recently returned from the mission field so we can view some of the things a missionary is trained to see as we inspect our churches together. With that, I would invite you to join me as we investigate our American Evangelical house with fresh eyes.

Chapter 2

Our Home and Its Hood

Contextualization in Familiar Landscapes

As I drove up North 6th Street to help prepare my childhood home for sale, I found myself looking at the familiar surroundings with a sense of nostalgia. At the same time as I remembered the place, I could also tell there had been changes. One home had new siding in a different color, while another had an expanded front porch. The car in the neighbor's driveway had a Florida license plate instead of the familiar Wisconsin plates, and several of the old Maple trees that lined the street had been reduced to stumps.

I realized I had assumed the place would still be the same as it was in my memory. *The Jones family lives next door in the brick house. They have three kids who are always up for a pick-up game of basketball. Across the street in the two-story house with white siding is where the eccentric high school English teacher lives. And of course,*

I know if my ball goes over the fence in the back alley into old lady Judith's yard, I will never get it back.

I assumed I still knew the neighbors, and still knew how to interact with them.

But the thing is, neighborhoods change. Sometimes those changes are obvious—for instance, the Jones family had moved away and a retired couple had moved in. Now the kids I had played with every day during the summer were no longer next door. In fact, they were no longer kids at all. The neighbor family who we considered to be our close friends had been replaced by new residents who were now our neighbors by mere accident of proximity.

Other times, however, the changes are less obvious. The neighbor girl had gone off to an Ivy League university, but I was unaware her parents had wanted her to go to a trade school. Now, unbeknownst to me, my casual conversation about the prestige of her school reminded her parents of their frustrated desires for their daughter. My remarks about how proud they must be introduced invisible tension into the conversation because my perception of the value of the university—assumed to be shared with the neighbors—actually differed from theirs.

These changes—both the obvious and the invisible—affect how people operate and how they relate to one another. Over time, they reshape and alter the culture of the neighborhood. Sometimes, such changes occur so slowly and imperceptibly that we continue operating as we always have only to find ourselves causing offense or acting inappropriately without being aware our habits are no longer acceptable. We tend to develop implicit ideas about the way things are on the basis of the way they have always been.

But the contexts in which we live are not static realities. For our words and actions to communicate what we intend them to communicate, we must make sure we are students of our own culture and context. Missionaries refer to this process as contextualization.

Missionary Lenses and Biblical Contextualization

When entering a new culture, it is easy to notice the overt differences from what was normal back home. For most missionaries, their training has prepared them to recognize local customs, to determine what is offensive and what is acceptable, and to note ways that language functions differently in their new setting. Noting these differences and the effect they have on relationships, missionaries diligently work to develop patterns of faithful communication of the unchanging content of the Bible within the changing contexts of the world. This, in admittedly simplistic terms, is what I mean by contextualization.

Contextualization is a basic expectation of cross-cultural missionary work that requires the development of skills of close observation, asking incisive questions, and reflecting theologically on how one can faithfully teach and apply biblical truth in a way that will be meaningful within an unfamiliar context. These skills have obvious cross-cultural benefits, but I would argue that they also need to be employed in familiar settings.

Some churches do attempt to find contextually sensitive ways to establish their connection to the community. They might serve locally roasted artisan coffee in the lobby, or choose to highlight compassion ministries in which they are involved that are part of the local concern. While these applications may be forms of contextualization, they do not necessarily address the first and most central task of contextual communication.

Contextualization done properly must first concern itself with assessing how the context will naturally understand the language and concepts used to proclaim the gospel. The purpose of such linguistic investigation is to identify where biblical *words* might currently mean less-than-biblical *things* to our neighbors. This communication task is one of the first areas where Lesslie Newbigin's missionary perspective is valuable to our task as disciple makers at home.

> **Contextualization done properly must first concern itself with assessing how the context will naturally understand the language and concepts used to proclaim the gospel.**

Lessons from Newbigin

When Lesslie Newbigin arrived in India and began learning the local tongue, he quickly encountered a perennial communication dilemma. The Tamil words he needed to share the gospel came laden with gospel-contradicting baggage. In what was one of Newbigin's final public addresses, he recounted the problem he faced throughout his years of ministry as he sought to communicate biblical truth in language saturated with Hindu thought, saying,

> I have done a good deal of street preaching in my life and I have often stood in a street to preach the gospel where the name of Jesus is unknown. . . . Of course I must find one of the many Tamil words for God and there are many words. And when I use one of those words, I know that in my hearer's minds they will be thinking perhaps Shea or Vishnu or Murugan or Subramanya or Ganesha or Hanuman. They will certainly not be thinking of the one whom I think of when I say the word God, the one I have learned to know through Jesus Christ.[1]

Often, in the context of missions, the words necessary and available to convey the basics of the biblical gospel come pre-loaded with meaning that runs contrary to the gospel message. This reality requires additional work to ensure the words the communicator uses are given biblical definition rather than assuming that shared vocabulary automatically communicates shared meaning.

---

1. Lesslie Newbigin, "Gospel and Culture" (December 1996), 113–21 in *Signs Amidst the Rubble*, ed. Geoffrey Wainwright (Grand Rapids: Eerdmans, 2003), 117.

As he encountered the distance between what he intended to communicate about the God of the Bible and the natural understanding of the words he needed to use, Newbigin did not abandon the biblical language that caused confusion. Rather, Newbigin appealed to the defining power of the biblical story to shape the reader's understanding of its terms. He writes,

> That is why—whether we are talking about our own culture or about another one—the crucial question is whether we tell the story, whether we continue to recount the mighty acts of God, whether we continue over and over and over again to read and reread and ponder the story of Jesus, because it is only the telling of the story that can change the meaning of the words we use and the concepts we entertain.[2]

It is noteworthy that this quote is drawn from the end of Newbigin's life when his labors in India began to bear fruit in his home country. He returned to the West asking, "How can the European churches, whose life and thought is shaped so completely by this post-Enlightenment culture, become bearers of a mission to that culture?"[3] Having had his life and ministry

---

2. Newbigin, "The Gospel and Culture," 118.
3. Newbigin, "The Cultural Captivity of Western Christianity," in *A Word in Season: Perspectives in Christian World Missions* (Grand Rapids: Eerdmans, 1994), 69. Or as he stated it in Newbigin, *Foolishness to the Greeks* (Grand Rapids: Eerdmans, 1986), 10, he asks, "From whence can the voice, not of doom but of deliverance, be spoken so that the modern Western world can hear it as the voice of its Savior and Lord?"

planted back in his home country for more than two decades, he recognized the need for defining our language biblically is as important when speaking English in the West as it is when speaking Tamil in India.

With Newbigin, I believe it is critical that American Christians learn to use the tools of contextualization at home. Just as someone returning to the home of their youth will need to become reacquaint with the neighborhood, so too will we need to freshly investigate the cultures around us if we want to meaningfully present the biblical gospel as the true center of the story of the universe. And, lest we think that contextualization is merely the concern of pastors and missionaries, we need to own this effort as an every-Christian endeavor as we all seek to communicate the unchanging gospel of Jesus Christ faithfully within a changing world.

Doing Contextualization at Home

If gospel communication is the necessary center of our disciple-making task, we must acquire contextual awareness. Contextual awareness helps us to identify and overcome potential barriers to understanding as we are speaking with our neighbors. While the need for such assessment is clear when one encounters the obvious barriers like different languages, it is perhaps less obvious when the cultures exhibit apparent similarities and shared vocabulary. Still, the cultures surrounding many American churches today—though speaking a common language—often understand the language of the gospel in ways stripped of its biblical meaning.

Consider the word *love* as an illustration of what I mean. In First John, we read several times the affirmation, "God is love." This is a central point of belief for Christians, and it is something that usually will not offend those outside of the Christian faith. But the lack of offense is because those words mean different things within American culture based on the ways they are more commonly used.

With just a little bit of reflection, we can find ample evidence to show how the word *love* has taken on extra-biblical and even anti-biblical meaning in our society. Consider the effect of the euphemism for sex, "making love." Under the influence of phrases such as this, our society has reduced the concept of love to something that is tightly associated with sexual expression. As a result, the phrase "God is love" is expanded by the sentiments more broadly available in the popular LGBTQ+ slogan, "Love is love." Many in our society believe that a God who is love must be affirming of any activities that the parties involved might identify as expressions of love.[4]

Though the Bible and the culture around us are using the same word here, we are faced with the same conundrum that Newbigin encountered in India. We could engage in the same exercise for any number of biblical terms that have been dislodged from their biblical setting and meaning through contemporary usage. Words like *sin, salvation, forgiveness, justification,* and *atonement* are all central to the expression of the gospel. But each one

---

4. To expand on this discussion, I would highly recommend the book by Rebecca McLaughlin, *The Secular Creed* (Austin, TX: TGC, 2021).

must be defined by its biblical context to ensure the intended meaning is received.

In order to help make these ideas more practical, I want to highlight three steps that missionaries take in cross-cultural engagements that can help us to understand our home cultures and how they have changed. These three steps are not necessarily linear, nor is this a task that one will ever complete. Contextualization requires ongoing assessment. But as we seek to communicate the unchanging message of the Bible within changing societies, it is important for us to dedicate ourselves to this task so as to make sure we continue to communicate clearly and faithfully the one message of hope entrusted to us.

Three-Step Contextualization

What follows is a very basic contextualization approach that I believe will prove helpful for conducting a fresh inspection of the cultures that our home churches inhabit. These three steps run parallel with Newbigin's three-part gospel communication proposal, though they are also common to most missionary engagements with new cultures.[5] Let me briefly explain the three steps

---

5. Newbigin, *Foolishness to the Greeks*, 5–6. Here he argues first that any true communication of the gospel must occur in language that is understandable. Second, the gospel will challenge and chasten its hearers as the biblical story and content confront nonbiblical culture and worldview. And third, any communication resulting in conversion is the work of God and not of clever human argument.

before considering three overarching ways to prepare ourselves as individuals and as churches to do this work in our local settings.

Step One: Observe and Inquire

Just like kids growing up in a familiar neighborhood, those who have spent their lives in the same context have likely adopted certain local norms in often unnoticed ways. These norms may be as simple as rooting for the same sports teams, or they may be as complex as adopting similar political opinions and social concerns. And sometimes fast and observable changes in society distract us from the slow and discrete worldview shifts that produced them.

For instance, before we left the United States, same-sex marriage was not legal in most states. By the time we returned to the United States in 2017, same-sex marriages were not only legal but had become so normalized that questioning this freedom was akin to hate speech. These were clear and broad-reaching societal changes that had quickly advanced across the American cultural landscape. In response, many Christians set to work defending biblical teaching on marriage, sex, and sexuality. Others found themselves asking, "How did we get here?"

There is a perennial necessity for helping Christians to understand and defend the biblical teaching on such issues as marriage, sex, and sexuality. However, a missionary will recognize there is more work to be done in helping Christians to engage with these ideas than merely equipping them with the ability to articulate biblical conclusions.[6] That is because missionaries encountering new cultural phenomena are trained to push beyond the phenomena themselves and into a deeper assessment of the underlying worldview.

Such overt and observable cultural shifts are merely the outcomes of more foundational cultural changes at the level of worldview. Before people can understand biblical truth, a Christian communicator should be attuned to the underlying presuppositions that create barriers to understanding the gospel. While the biblical truths are timeless and applicable to everyone, not everyone is immediately attuned to their need for this message. In order to discover where a person might be open to the message of the gospel, Christians will benefit from learning about how this person sees the world. To do so, they must ask certain key questions.[7]

> In order to discover where a person might be open to the message of the gospel, Christians will benefit from learning about how this person sees the world.

---

6. Much ink has been spilled, many blogs have been written, and sundry sermons have been preached which defend the biblical teaching on marriage and sex as being designed for one man and one woman. I believe these traditional interpretations of biblical teaching on marriage, sex, and sexuality have been adequately demonstrated and defended elsewhere, so I don't intend to rehash the particulars here.

7. See for example, James Sire, *The Universe Next Door*, 6th ed. (Downers Grove, IL: IVP Academic, 2020); see also the inclusion of questions similar to the ones I have used here as woven throughout the multi-volume work of

Let me briefly list and explain the worldview questions I think are vital to observing and inquiring about how our friends view the world. I will primarily focus on the answers that might be given by secular materialists as this perspective is increasingly pervasive in the Western world.[8] However, the questions are pertinent to exploring any number of theistic worldviews as well. We will then consider how these questions can provoke further reflection and even open up opportunity for inviting people to hear the biblical answers through the story Scripture tells.

Where Are We? (Where did everything come from? Why does something exist instead of nothing?) Everyone on earth today is living out of various implicit assumptions regarding the answers to the question, "What is this place?" But having to articulate those assumptions can tell us a lot about how a person views the world and their place in it. The story a person believes about the origins of the universe will dramatically shape the way they understand its purpose, trajectory, and value.

Who Are We? (What does it mean to be human? Why are people valuable?) The idea of human identity is another area that is universally important. Is there something that makes human beings distinct from animals and other living things? If so, what

---

N. T. Wright, *Christian Origins and the Question of God,* 4 vols. (Minneapolis, MN: Fortress, 1992–2013).

8. By secular materialists, I simply refer to those who function according to the assumption that the material world and its observable patterns are all that can really be counted as true. This is a broader category than those who would identify themselves as atheists or agnostics. A secular materialist might acknowledge the reality of the spiritual aspect of a person without affirming any objective truth is found therein.

is the basis for this distinction? How do your neighbors understand and defend the claim that every person has inherent human dignity?

What Is Wrong? (Why is there suffering and pain in the world? Why is there evil?) Suffering is a pervasive reality in our world. No one can escape it. There are very few who would not immediately associate suffering and pain with evil and brokenness. But what causes such evil and pain? What is wrong with the world, and why do people hurt one another so often? And, for that matter, what makes bad things *bad*? How can this unfortunate situation be explained?

What Is the Solution? (Is there any hope of making it better? How do we fix what is broken?) Related to the previous question about what is wrong is the hope that whatever is wrong can be made right. Is the solution external to a person or internal? Do they believe themselves to be complicit in or victims of the world's problems? Asking our neighbors what they think would provide relief from suffering or bring an end to evil can provide significant insight into their hopes, values, and desires.

Why Do We Exist? (What is the purpose or goal of life? How do we know if we are successful?) As one gets a glimpse of where their neighbor's hopes for a solution lie, the answers to the question of purpose are not far behind. As people express their hopes for a solution to their experience of suffering, there is opportunity to imagine a world in which frustrations, evil, and suffering are no more. This leads naturally into the question of "What then? How would the relief of suffering allow you to achieve your goals and make your life count?"

Step Two: Expose and Provoke

Learning to ask these five questions can go a long way to engaging in meaningful observation and assessment of one's surrounding culture. It allows for people to express in their own words the way they understand the world and their place in it. By listening well to their answers, we have the opportunity to hear how our neighbors use their language and what they mean by it. By listening, we will begin to recognize where the words and concepts that our friends use differently will need to be biblically redefined in order to ensure true gospel-communication.

At the same time, such questions can expose inconsistencies in how our neighbors view the world that have gone uninspected. Thus, these inquiries often provoke reflection on what alternatives might relieve such inconsistency. Consider the following brief examples of how those from various worldviews might articulate answers to these universal questions.

Atheists/Materialists: Where Are We?

The hard sciences have contributed to our understanding of how the regular features of our world work. For many of our neighbors, the confidence that scientific observation affords us regarding the regularity of these laws of physics has trickled over into metaphysical claims—that is, claims about the nature of existence, and what lies beneath reality. But science has made claims about metaphysics that it cannot substantiate. Though scientific observation of repeatable events in nature can predict *how* the world will act, it cannot offer insight into *why* the universe exists.

Still, many whose confidence in science has led them to a materialist understanding of the world deny the universe has its source in any intelligent creator. Instead, they propose that today's universe owes its origin to random and unguided development over an indeterminate amount of time. Where did the world come from? A materialist must appeal to an infinite regress of cause and effect in a universe composed of eternally existent matter. In so doing, they undermine their ability to speak about the *purpose* of the universe.

Newbigin helpfully summarizes this as he writes, "Cause is something that can be discovered by observation and reason. Purpose is not available for inspection because, until the purpose has been realized, it is hidden in the mind of the one whose purpose it is."[9]

In addition to the unsatisfying nature of this proposal, if there is no designer, then there is no design. If there is no design, then there is no purpose. If there is no purpose, then there are no grounds for assessing actions as good or bad, right or wrong. If there are no grounds for assessing good, bad, right, and wrong, then it is impossible to determine whether or not one's choices are meaningful, valuable, or fruitful apart from one's own ungrounded estimation of their value. Without a purposeful creator, the universe can have no meaning.

---

9. Lesslie Newbigin, *Proper Confidence: Faith, Doubt, and Certainty in Christian Discipleship* (Grand Rapids: Eerdmans, 1995), 57.

Purposeless origins produce a meaningless present and a worthless future. All of a sudden, atheism/materialism is seen to lack the resources to helpfully answer *any* of our questions. Exposed to this reality, our friends and neighbors might be provoked to revisit their assumptions about what science can and cannot tell us about the world and our place in it.

Pluralists/Agnostics: Who Are We?

As a part of the material world, the question of human identity is naturally connected to the previous question. Yet when it is asked of our Western neighbors, most people will appeal not to human origins, but to individual experience and self-determined identity. Agnostics and pluralists may suggest humans could be the creation of a higher power, but in the end, most agnostics are prone to gather a collection of the circumstances of their birth, communally acquired affinities, and self-determined assertions as a way of identifying themselves.

For instance, someone might answer a question of identity with a series of descriptions, such as "I am a straight, white, married, Christian male who is an American, a professor, and a Chicago Bears fan." All of those adjectives describe features of a person's life, but they fall short of defining the humanity of the person. We know this implicitly because if any one of those adjectives were exchanged for a different descriptor, the human identity would remain.

But if our friends contend that humans have inherent dignity, then there must be a more substantive ground for identity than mere description and self-identification of individuals. Here, the biblical account of God's special creation of image-bearing humans provides a foil against which to compare any alternative claims to why the claim of inherent human dignity might be sustained. The question of what makes a human important and valuable can thus expose a deep inconsistency in a pluralist's worldview while also provoking a search for a firmer foundation to the idea of human dignity.

Jews/Muslims: What Is Wrong and What Is the Solution?

In addressing the source of human dignity, the Christian communicator has the chance to present human beings as creatures whose identity, allegiance, and duty are bound up in the purposes of the Creator whose image they bear. This has immediate implications. What is right and good emerges from the givenness of humanity's divinely assigned purpose. In contrast, that which deviates from this purpose is to be identified as wrong.

In Judaism and Islam God contains no imperfections and is inherently good. But if God is perfect and righteous, and if he is also just and holy, then he cannot comingle with the unholy, impure, and guilty. And if this God has created in order to dwell with his image-bearing people—as the Bible repeatedly records— then his approach poses a grave danger to humans who are marred by their imperfections and rebellion.

If we admit that all humans are sinful and broken, then entering the presence of a holy and righteous God is a terrifying reality. The only way for us to dwell with this God, then, is for us to undergo a radical removal of our sin, guilt, impurity, and rebellion. Neither Judaism nor Islam provides such a solution. Even though both use the language of forgiveness, purification, and even atonement, neither faith includes a means for immediate and unmediated human interaction with God. Their proposed solutions to the sin problem produce a dissatisfying vision of hope for image-bearers designed for the presence of the God whose image they bear.

Individualists: Why Do We Exist?

As we surface the reality of human suffering and proposals for its alleviation, we naturally come to the question of ultimate purpose. If one could solve all the world's problems, then what would come next? For many in the West who have been raised to think of people as fully autonomous individuals, the removal of suffering would result in allowing everyone to pursue whatever they determine to make them happy.

But reality and experience demonstrate that happiness is fickle and fleeting. What makes a person feel happy one day might not satisfy the next. Furthermore, as is often the case, one person's happiness is the source of another's misery. For example, when I got married to my wife, I experienced happiness, while her other suitors experienced disappointment! Can we really hang our hopes for a meaningful life on something so demonstrably unstable and inequitable as our pursuit of happiness?

Step Three: Invite and Apply

At this point in the conversation, having asked good questions and listened to the answers, we are better equipped to speak meaningfully due to having a more intimate knowledge of how our friends view the world. These questions may have opened up an opportunity to expose dissatisfaction or highlight inconsistencies for our neighbors and their worldview. Likewise, we may have heard our friends using words in ways that diverge from how they would be used in presenting a biblical worldview.

All of this helps to orient us to the immediate context in front of us: our neighbors and their understanding of the world. Likewise, rather than simply offering a tract with isolated Bible verses that may or may not touch on the concerns raised by our friends, this approach offers us the opportunity to invite someone to see what the Bible says in response to any given question. This does, however, require us to be intimately familiar with the whole story of Scripture, so we can jump in at any given point and demonstrate how these questions find their ultimate answers in the gospel.

This brings us to one of the most challenging but helpful statements Newbigin makes about the concept of contextualization: *the task of contextualization is not figuring out how to infuse biblical teaching into a culture, but rather how to bring a culture to infuse itself with the biblical story.* He writes,

> Authentic Christian thought and action begin
> not by attending to the aspirations of the people,
> not by answering the questions they are asking

in their terms, not by offering solutions to the problems as the world sees them. It must begin and continue by attending to what God has done in the story of Israel and supremely in the story of Jesus Christ. It must continue by indwelling that story so that it is our story, the way we understand the real story. And then, and this is the vital point, to attend with open hearts and minds to the real needs of people in the way that Jesus attended to them, knowing that the real need is that which can only be satisfied by everything that comes from the mouth of God (Matt. 4:4).[10]

As we ask questions of our neighbors, we will realize there are multiple places where their worldviews offer insufficient answers. But rather than accommodating the biblical message to the stories they tell, the task of contextualization as Newbigin sees it is to show how the biblical story subverts every other story of the world.

Faithful contextualization is not the retrofitting of biblical concepts into existing cultural structures. It is rather finding places where a culture's story is ready to be abandoned in favor of the biblical story. However, as we see the Word of God confronting and displacing the stories told outside of the church, it likewise demands conformity from the stories told inside of

---

10. Lesslie Newbigin, *The Gospel in a Pluralist Society* (Grand Rapids: Eerdmans, 1989), 151.

the church. It will expose ways that the church has imbibed the cultural stories more than it has embodied the biblical narrative. Inevitably, allowing the biblical story to challenge all other stories will be quite dangerous to our comfort.

Our Churches: Contextualization or Compromise?

As Newbigin helped his Indian Christian friends see the danger of confusion and syncretism that attended their Hindu-saturated language and practices, he also began to discover ways that his own practices had been culturally shaped. He testifies to this reality in an address titled, "The Cultural Captivity of Western Christianity," where he writes,

> When I went as a young missionary to India, I could find the elements of syncretism in Indian Christianity. I saw how, inevitably, the meaning of sentences spoken by my Christian friends was shaped by the Hindu background of the language. The words used, the only available words for God, sin, salvation, and so on, are words that have received their entire content from the Hindu religious tradition. . . . Only slowly did I come to see that my own Christianity was also profoundly syncretistic.[11]

---

11. Lesslie Newbigin, "The Cultural Captivity of Western Christianity," 68.

In the same way as Hindus who simply add Jesus to their temples fall into syncretism, so too are Westerners susceptible when they attempt to fit Jesus into their materialism, nationalism, or individualism.

As this investigation continues, we will find that such an approach will challenge and even offend all of us, exposing places that the world's stories have crept in alongside of the biblical story. Whether we are prone to nationalism or critical of it, whether we are tempted by materialism, or appalled by it, all of us need to be recalibrated according to the gospel and its story. All of our lesser stories and the idols at the center of them will be challenged when the Bible's story truly comes to reign in our thinking, living, worshipping, and fellowshipping. As we read Newbigin's admission of his own syncretism, we might find ourselves shocked, but his honest assessment of his practice provides a good prompt for our own self-reflection.

Later in his ministry, Newbigin observed this naïvete to one's own contextual conditioning is not a problem unique to his experience. Following a visit to America and working with churches there, Newbigin reflected, "Conservative evangelicals were often unaware of the cultural conditioning of their religion and therefore guilty, as many of them now realize, of confusing the gospel with the values of the American way of life without realizing what they were doing."[12] Though he observed this tendency in the American church decades ago, it is worth considering whether or not it remains today.

---

12. Newbigin, *Foolishness to the Greeks*, 2.

Newbigin's missionary perspective caused him to conclude that the missionary "sees his own culture with the Christian eyes of a foreigner, and the foreigner can see what the native cannot see. We do not see the lenses of our spectacles; we see through them, and it is another who has to say to us, 'Friend, you need a new pair of spectacles.'"[13] Throughout the following chapters, as we borrow Newbigin's missionary spectacles, we will likely discover some of the ways that embracing our American context may distort or obscure the fullness of biblical teaching. May it be that through this endeavor we would don missionary lenses and in so doing welcome the Lord's critique of how our churches may have allowed our context to influence the way we go about the task of believing, living, and proclaiming the unchanging message of our crucified and risen King Jesus.

13. Newbigin, "The Cultural Captivity of Western Christianity," 66–69.

Chapter 3

Our Dining Room

Diverse Ministry as Embodied Apologetic

W hat I experienced as I walked into my childhood home after being away for so long was like one of those scenes from a movie where the character is surrounded by swirling memories of people and events that took place in that space in years gone by. Walking in, I was greeted by the stairs leading to the second floor. I could still remember which ones squeaked and needed to be avoided in order to make a successful midnight raid on the kitchen while my parents slept.

In front of me was the hallway leading to the kitchen. As I entered, my memory caught whiffs of snickerdoodle cookies being baked in the oven and the smell of my dad sautéing mushrooms for Saturday morning omelets. The nostalgic smile on my face turned into a chuckle as I rounded the corner and saw the laundry chute in the wall into which I always imagined dropping my sisters when I was angry at them. Next to the laundry chute hung the heavy swinging door that led into the dining room.

As I stepped into the small space of the dining room, I found I was surrounded by what some might call "clutter." There was an upright piano nestled in one corner and a curio cabinet in another. Bookshelves stood along the wall, and a stereo table under the window had various decorations strewn across its surface. This stuff formed an outer hedge around the room that made it feel even more cramped than its square footage might suggest. Much of the stuff would need to be removed in order to highlight the seating capacity of the room as we staged it for presentation.

In the center of the room, however, was the dining room table that my parents had owned since they'd gotten married. This table had taken a beating during its two decades in that room, but the marks it bore in its varnished finish served as evidence of its use. The thing that I remember about this table was that, despite the cramped room in which it sat, there were three extra table leaves in storage behind the swinging door. These three leaves were regularly brought out to extend the table's capacity to accommodate the various guests who joined us for meals.

What was striking was that somehow, despite how small the room was, it never felt cramped to add those extra leaves. Chairs would be brought in from around the house and guests would settle in to enjoy the rich fellowship that comes when Christians do the daily work of breaking bread together, rehashing their days, laughing, crying, and praying around the table.

In the act of adding those leaves my parents showed my sisters and me the value of believing that there is always enough room around the table. By intentionally hosting people from various walks of life, we also got a front row seat to how the gospel truly makes us family with people from very different backgrounds. At that table we grew in our ability to listen well to the experiences of these brothers and sisters from various places and prerogatives as we learned to appreciate the beautiful diversity of God's family.

That dining room served our family much like the sanctuary, fellowship hall, and community of the church can serve a neighborhood as a workshop for and display of Christian unity. When people who come from different backgrounds gather, such a display of an otherwise-uncommon unity provides an embodied apologetic for the gospel.

Sometimes, though, we get distracted by all the extra stuff we pile into the room. In so doing, we fool ourselves into acting like there is less room around the table than there is. One such way the American church is currently being distracted from celebrating around our high-capacity table is the way we respond to the contemporary discussions concerning race and ethnic tension in our country.

Admittedly, these conversations are highly charged. Individuals who misspeak on these issues are often publicly humiliated and condemned by people on all sides. Furthermore, the sociological resources to which people have recently been appealing are hotly contested and variously understood. Pastors and church members can become reticent to engage in these discussions due to the perceived dangers of offending or due to unfamiliarity with the implications of the language commonly used.

In this brief chapter I admit up front that there is no way to do justice to all the complexities surrounding race and ethnicity. Nonetheless, I do want to argue that our missionary lenses can help us to see past some of the clutter surrounding these issues. As we do, we will see the value of working to manifest a biblically driven and gospel-displaying unity for a world that is trying in vain to manufacture it. My goal in this chapter is to encourage racism-weary and race-leery Christians that these conversations are important. And I want to contend that the church has a unique reason for confidence in fighting for unity amidst diversity.

Observing the Clutter: The American Discussion about Race

We were overseas when the 2014 shooting of Michael Brown in Ferguson, Missouri, hit the American news cycle. Very quickly thereafter, this otherwise-obscure, mid-sized, Midwestern city quickly became a focus of global attention as protestors and rioters streamed into the streets in anger, frustration, and revolt. Some perceived the unrest as more than just a response to the shooting of Michael Brown—they saw it as the result of long-simmering tensions between law enforcement and people of color in Ferguson.[1] Since then, the United States has watched a heart-wrenching parade of similar stories that have highlighted the

---

1. See for example, D. A. Horton, *Intensional: Kingdom Ethnicity in a Divided World* (Colorado Springs: NavPress, 2019), 1.

untimely deaths of black men and women at the hands of local law enforcement.

Such stories continue to prove for many observers that communities of color are unfairly disadvantaged and targeted by people in power. Furthermore, many have become convinced that not only are individuals guilty of leveraging their power in racist fashion, but the structures and systems of our country that are designed to ensure security, the potential for economic progress, and the free pursuit of individual happiness have been indelibly corrupted by the stain and inequity of racist biases. Popularized versions of what is known as Critical Race Theory (CRT) permeate social media and teach that those with power and privilege have unfairly received such power and privilege by means of racist systems that perpetuate racially determined power imbalances.[2]

In an effort to try to correct these power dynamics, some have proposed seemingly radical solutions to deconstruct the existing structures and systems in order to rebuild more equitably from the ground up. Proposals to defund the police, reject capitalism, and ensure the support of every American to exhibit their own self-determined self-expression are topics of broad political debate. From legal theory to the teaching of history and to managing

---

2. For example, in June 2021, an address at Yale University sparked viral social media reflection and extreme applications of CRT principles. See Lateshia Beachum, "Yale Speaker Says Comment about Killing White People Was Meant to Spark Deeper Talk about Race," *Washington Post*, June 9, 2021, https://www.washingtonpost.com/education/2021/06/09/yale-lecturer-talks-about-killing-white-people/.

economic structures, the language of CRT has permeated much of the American dialogue about race.

As these discussions have moved into the church from their origins in broader society, many Christians have been at a loss for how to think and speak about race and racism in America. Some Christians have tried to critically engage the ideas and insights of CRT from a biblical perspective.[3] Some, however, have taken up polarizing positions on CRT. Some who affirm it as a necessary analytical tool accuse those who are skeptical of CRT of being closet racists. Some who reject CRT altogether label those who are open to using it as Marxists. The rhetoric—especially as displayed on social media—is often fiery and rarely charitable.[4]

I am convinced that much of the church's contemporary discussion about and reaction to CRT proves to be the clutter that makes our dining room feel cramped. Furthermore, many pastors

---

3. While CRT is not the primary focus of his work, I find the recent book by Carl Truman, *The Rise and Triumph of the Modern Self* (Wheaton, IL: Crossway, 2020), especially 225–68, to be a very helpful investigation of the many streams of influence that have laid the groundwork for critical theory in general and for critical race theory in particular where he treats them. I would also recommend the brief work of Rebecca McLaughlin, *The Secular Creed* (Austin, TX: TGC, 2021), to provide a fair treatment of some of the more popular manifestations and movements that lean on critical theory such as Black Lives Matter and the LGBTQ+ movement. Another helpful volume in the same vein is Thaddeus Williams, *Confronting Injustice without Compromising Truth* (Grand Rapids: Zondervan, 2020).

4. I have wrestled with the decision about whether or not to "name names" in these paragraphs referencing "some" whose opinions mark the poles of the spectrum. I am opting not to identify those whose work I find to be unhelpfully polarizing for the sake of neither mischaracterizing them via a label nor promoting the consumption of material I find to be ultimately unhelpful.

find themselves tempted to either uncritically embrace prevailing social theories or to avoid the discussions altogether. Rather than wading into an analysis of CRT of my own in this chapter, I want to call us to step back from the wide-ranging secular discussions about race and ask the question, "What resources might the church already possess to assess the world around us and confront places of racial injustice where we find them?" As we do so while intentionally donning our missionary lenses, we will also need to ask the question, "What might it say to a watching world if we as the church were leading the charge toward unity amidst diversity?"

As noted above, this chapter does not intend to answer all the important questions raised by American history or contemporary national tensions. Instead, the more modest goal of these pages is to remind those pastors and church members who are reticent to engage in such complex issues that the church has both theological and missiological reasons to fight for unity amidst diversity. As we consider these issues, we find that Lesslie Newbigin again provides for us an important example of this gospel-driven pursuit to display an uncommon unity.

> **The church has both theological and missiological reasons to fight for unity amidst diversity.**

Newbigin, India, and Gospel Unity

Even if you don't know much about India or Indian culture, it is likely you are familiar with the idea of the caste system. In brief, the caste system is a social hierarchy into which a person is inescapably born and assigned a station for life. Each caste comes with its own set of expectations, responsibilities, and protocols for relating to those of higher or lower castes. People do not associate socially with those above or below them, and according to traditional Hindu thought, the only way to escape one's caste assignment is to die and be reincarnated into another life station. While technically the caste system has been abolished, its influence persists in the practical outworking of social interactions in many parts of India to this day.

A central component of the missionary task is the proclamation of the gospel message that confronts and challenges social distinctions and hierarchies with the equality that is found at the foot of the cross.[5] For Newbigin, then, the issue of caste was immediately consequential for his work of planting churches whose composition was not socially determined, but was the result of people in a shared location converting to faith in Jesus.[6] If someone from a low caste came to believe in Jesus, then the other higher caste believers in that place needed to wrestle with the implications of being members of a single spiritual family with those they previously had been trained to ignore, despise, and marginalize.

Despite what would today seem obviously wrong-headed, some of Newbigin's missionary colleagues suggested that the

---

5. See, for example, Colossians 3:11 and Galatians 3:28.

6. Newbigin was fond of referring to the local church as "the Church *for that place*," which has significant implications for how individual churches posture themselves in relation to the communities in which they reside. See Geoffrey Wainwright, *Lesslie Newbigin: A Theological Life* (Eugene, OR: Wipf & Stock, 2000), 118. See also, Paul Weston, *Lesslie Newbigin: Missionary Theologian* (Grand Rapids: Eerdmans, 2006), 133.

easiest way to see the gospel take root in India would be to start a high-caste church and a separate low-caste church to accommodate the cultural expectations and to retain natural kinship connections for new believers. They argued that the sociological barriers that needed to be crossed for a high-caste believer to fellowship meaningfully and fully with a believer from a lower caste were too high to try to leap. Newbigin, however, could not reconcile the unifying message of the gospel with a vision of churches that were intentionally built along sociological divides.

This vision of unity in the gospel was labeled by some of his colleagues as a naïve idealism or as an unnecessary hindrance to the speed of church growth. Newbigin highlights this as he comments,

> The missiologists of the "Church Growth" school deplore [mixing castes] and insist that—as a matter of missionary obedience—the Church should accept and welcome the organization of congregations of different castes in the same town or city. Most Indian Christians would utterly repudiate this suggestion as, in present conditions, a denial of the Gospel (rightly I believe).[7]

---

7. Wainwright, *Lesslie Newbigin: Missionary Theologian*, 119. Admittedly, Newbigin concludes this thought by making a temporary exception for churches dealing with ethnic tensions. His intention here, however, is to ensure that various bodies of ethnically similar believers who would represent a minority in established churches be allowed to develop a maturity in their faith prior to being subsumed by a congregation composed of an ethnic majority. While there are certainly unique factors to be considered, I would

By fighting for a caste-blended church, Newbigin was not pursuing a naïve and impractical idealism. Rather, he simply trusted the gospel was a strong enough spiritual message that it could overcome the material and social opposition it faced.

Convinced that the unity the gospel creates should manifest itself in the diverse fellowship of believers from all social distinctions, Newbigin confidently insisted that the one gospel creates one people whose core commonality outstrips any superficial differences. He makes this point powerfully, writing,

> Where is the centripetal force strong enough to hold together the communities drawn [apart] by the centrifugal power of their separate ethnic and religious identities[?] . . . The good news [is] that in the atoning work of Jesus Christ there is provided for us all that place, that "mercy seat" where we can be reconciled to one another because we have been reconciled to God.[8]

For Newbigin, the atonement that grafts alien branches into a single root testifies to a stronger unifying force than the forces that would separate us according to our differences.

It is worth noting that despite his optimism about this unified vision of the local church, Newbigin does not deny the distinct cultures and social locations of the various subcultures with whom

---

contend that if there are racial tensions in the community, the church cannot remain satisfied in an intentionally segregated condition if it is truly to be a church for that place.

8. As cited in Wainwright, *Lesslie Newbigin: A Theological Life*, 133.

he was working. Neither does he suppose that such a diverse community will be easily freed of the existing external tensions between such groups. He simply committed himself to the belief that the kingdom of God into which believers of all backgrounds are saved is singular. Thus, members of the kingdom must work together as a manifestation of their shared allegiances—even while knowing that their work toward such unity will be marked by difficulty and will never bring about a full kingdom realization this side of the new creation. He writes,

> The perfect society cannot lie this side of death.
> And moreover it cannot be the direct result of
> our efforts. We all rightly shrink from the phrase,
> "building the Kingdom of God" not because the
> kingdom does not call for our labor, but because
> we know that the best work of our hands and
> brains is too much marred by egotism and pride
> and impure ambition to be itself fit for the king-
> dom. All our social institutions, even the very
> best that have been produced under Christian
> influence, have still the taint of sin about them.
> By their own horizontal development they can-
> not, as it were, become the Kingdom of God.[9]

This presently imperfect realization did not deter Newbigin, however. Local churches will always be composed of people who

---

9. Lesslie Newbigin, *Signs Amidst the Rubble* (Grand Rapids: Eerdmans, 2003), 46–47.

are yet struggling against their own sins of prejudice and preference, yet Newbigin saw gospel-centered unity across demographic
divides as a foreshadowing of the kingdom as it will one day be.
When a local church displays such an uncommon unity, it provides an embodied apologetic and reinforces the power of the
gospel.

Missiology and Diversity Discussions Today

The prioritization of speedy exigencies over the long work
of manifesting gospel reconciliation among diverse people groups
is not something that was unique
to Newbigin's day. It is something
that is wrestled with on the mission
field today—perhaps to an even
greater degree than when Newbigin
clashed with church growth movement advocates. In fact, this was
something I heard on the mission
field within the last decade.

> **Local churches will
> always be composed
> of people who
> are yet struggling
> against their own
> sins of prejudice
> and preference.**

One of the problems we faced
in our ministry in the Middle East
was how best to help believers from a Muslim background enter
into fellowship with those from a Christian background. As I
sought outside counsel, I was told by a well-respected missionary
strategist, "You should just start two different kinds of churches—
one for Muslim background believers and one for Christian background believers. It will slow things down too much if these new

believers have to work through all the historical and cultural baggage that comes from bringing former persecutors into the community they persecuted."

To be honest, I was stunned by the answer. I asked him later in the day if I had heard him correctly when he said we should not encourage believers from a Muslim background to fellowship with those believers who grew up culturally as Christians. He confirmed that I had heard him correctly: start two different kinds of churches because there is too much baggage to hope for unity.

This was a man who had overseen some reportedly incredible movements of people to Christ in another context. He had been brought into our training as an expert missiologist. But his advice to avoid dealing with conflict within the fellowship of believers was grossly dissatisfying—both theologically and practically. To be honest, the more I reflected on it, the more frustrated I got. The pragmatism reflected in this advice was being allowed to trump the beauty of the enemy-reconciling effect of the gospel. I mean, think about it: What would have been the result for the early church if in Acts 9 Ananias had refused to receive Saul because of the sociological tension that it would cause to fellowship with a former persecutor?

These sentiments, however, aren't exclusive to the mission field. I also had a disappointing experience in a classroom in the United States once when a Christian professor dismissed the discussion about multiethnic churches altogether. His comment was that this is just a fad that is responding to contemporary sensitivities and that churches would do better to stay culturally homogeneous. He said, "I mean, multiethnic worship is a fine idea until your church service lasts three hours and people are hooting and hollering over your shoulder throughout the whole service."

Is it true that bringing together different communities might require each community to begin to appreciate expressions and forms of worship that are not native to their subculture? Certainly. But is the potential for discomfort sufficient reason to not pursue fellowship with brothers and sisters who share a common faith and theology? Hardly. What is lost if segregation of churches remains a practice of convenience? We lose multiple opportunities to learn from one another as we seek to live out a shared faith in different circumstances. And we lose multiple opportunities to display to a watching world how compelling the fellowship of the gospel is.

A few years after the disappointing advice from the missiologist, however, I got a taste of what could happen if we didn't allow socially-defined distinctions to determine the composition of our fellowship. I had been given the privilege of getting to teach a church planting course in an underground Bible school. The twenty-or-so students who composed the class came from various Christian upbringings, and some had come to faith in Jesus out of Muslim families. Some of those of a Muslim background were even connected to high-ranking government and military officials who would have been responsible for overseeing various waves of targeted persecution of Christians throughout their country.

Standing in front of the classroom and observing small groups of those diverse students huddled together and strategizing about how they might link arms and plant churches together was one of the most stunning displays of the unifying power of the gospel I have ever seen. Those who were formerly aligned with persecutors were collaborating with those whose families had encountered persecution. And the only thing that brought them together was a common gospel-given identity and goal. The pain and history they shared was not erased or forgotten. But the gospel was sufficient to call both parties to walk through the painful history toward repentance and forgiveness and to continue working together toward a shared vision of the future on the basis of a present understanding of the gospel they held in common.

As those communities began to work toward planting churches, their friendship, fellowship, and partnership displayed the healing power of the gospel. It was not unlikely that there would be conflict and tension along the way. Still, that they were drawn together by a common task and vision testifies to the reconciling power of a shared gospel identity. This unity is encouraging to those sharing in the fellowship, and it is compelling to those observing from the outside.

So how does all of this discussion relate to contemporary American churches and their approach to addressing ethnic tensions? From the outset, I hope it gives us a confidence in three things:

1. We are all sin-stained and in need of reconciliation to God and then to one another as God's people.

2. The community of believers draws confidence in the work of reconciliation to one another that comes from a shared reconciliation to God.

3. The secular world is attempting to manufacture human unity without a compelling
reason to believe it is possible.

Yet as they observe the church manifesting and enjoying a unity amidst diversity, they have to stop and marvel. But it will take intentional work.

Manifesting Unity: Three Recommendations

Newbigin's conviction to pursue unity required no consultation with prevailing sociological theories. He did not need to appeal to any extra-biblical data to find the reason and resources to fight for unity amidst diversity in the local church. That is because Newbigin was rightly convinced by Paul's logic in Romans 11 that the gospel grafts believers into the solitary vine of Christ, thus creating one family from the disparate and divided families of the earth.[10] He was enraptured by the consistent biblical vision of a single people of God composed of all the nations, tribes, and tongues of the earth that is highlighted from Genesis 12 through to Revelation 21.

Christians—of all people—have the theological reasons and resources available to fight for and fight from the ultimate unity they share in Christ. And missiologically, when Christians embody such a diverse unity, a fractured world takes notice. Onlookers

---

10. One might also consider the unifying imagery of being made the temple of God as seen in Ephesians 2:11–22 or the body of Christ as in 1 Corinthians 12:12–31.

observe something curiously beautiful when people choose to assemble as a congregation composed of individuals from communities that are hostile to one another. And when the diverse members of that church disburse from the weekly gathering and still choose to intentionally seek out fellowship together in one another's neighborhoods, backyards, and dining rooms, such friendships are noteworthy.

> **The gospel grafts believers into the solitary vine of Christ, thus creating one family from the disparate and divided families of the earth.**

The gospel gives Christians the confidence that such unity ultimately already exists at the most fundamental level among brothers and sisters in Christ. Our task, then, is not making or manufacturing such unity, but manifesting it. Still, there are some specific steps we can take to draw upon that unity for the benefit of our local body and for those looking in from the outside. The following three recommendations come from putting on missionary lenses and considering the issues of ethnic tension in the US from a missiological perspective.

Invite the Neighbors: Prioritize Local

Some of the questions we find ourselves dealing with as we seek to address the issues of racial tension in our churches come from conversations taking place nationally. Now, as I alluded to above, I do think it is wise for Christians and church leaders to pay attention to discussions happening outside of our own contexts. Nonetheless, it should be our priority to address any tensions in our own context prior to concerning ourselves with issues in other communities.

This reality was illustrated for us as we worked through issues of socially divided Christ followers overseas. Believers from historically Christian populations were prone to circulating stories of betrayal by purported believers of Muslim backgrounds who had infiltrated congregations only to serve as government informants. The fear, distrust, and genuine hurt caused by such events was real and could not be papered over. However, these regional stories often colored the initial interactions between long-time Christians and new converts from Muslim backgrounds in ways that hampered unity among local populations.

The healthiest relationships we saw between existing churches and new believers from Muslim backgrounds were built upon purposeful, humble, and direct engagement with one another as individuals. Addressing concerns and potential misunderstandings directly and for the purpose of fellowshipping together, these local believers slowly forged trust in one another despite the regional reasons to maintain their distance. The gospel-effected unity instantiated by local churches should lead believers to prioritize listening to the individuals in their midst to address the local and unique tensions facing their communities.

In the end, while the national discussions about American history and present issues are important, local churches need to begin their reconciliation work with the community in which they reside. It was Newbigin's conviction that a church in a place was to be a church first and foremost for that place. As such, churches should aim to engage and reflect the demographic realities of their communities and to minister in ways that prioritize addressing local needs.

In order to move from the ethereal realm of ideals to the practical level of actual ministry, it can be helpful to begin inspecting our local situations by means of probing questions. Here are a couple I have found helpful in assessing various places I have lived, both as a missionary overseas and as a member of American churches.

First, if there is a population segment that is present in your community but not in your membership, this would be an occasion to ask, "Is there something about our church and its ministry that is unwelcoming to this group?"

Second, as one of my colleagues asks, "Is there a part of town that we would hesitate to go in order to invite people to join us at church?"

These questions can help us see our communities in the way that missionaries look at theirs to determine where the gospel might encounter local boundaries that need to be overcome. Likewise, such questions can expose parts of our hearts that might be silently harboring prejudices or preferences that are cause for repentance.

These questions can help local churches open their eyes to the community around them. But once a diverse membership has gathered and joined in the fellowship, the work of manifesting and celebrating our united diversity is not over. In fact, this is where the more daily and difficult parts begin. We must intentionally invest time and energy to listen, hear, and understand one another with the aim of ministering to and with one another amidst our differences.

Expand the Table: Listening and Hearing Well

In any given city one is likely to observe the human tendency to trend toward homogeneity or similarity—be that socioeconomic, ethnic, or otherwise. In fact, from Newbigin's day to ours, missionaries have noted this tendency and come to refer to it as the Homogeneous Unit Principle (HUP).[11] In more colloquial idiom, it is the recognition that birds of a feather flock together.

If a church is to minister to its city as a whole—including all the diverse segments of its composition—its members will need to intentionally transcend those enclaves that all too easily form around our natural affinities. That will be best accomplished by forging interpersonal relationships that are not limited to convenience and proximity. It will mean inviting people from other neighborhoods to join us for meals in our homes and backyards. It will mean bringing our families to their homes and enjoying

---

11. Among the first to utilize these insights in developing a missionary strategy around what would later be labeled the HUP is the wildly influential Donald McGavran, *Bridges of God: A Study in the Strategy of Missions* (New York: Friendship Press, 1955), 23, who wrote, "Peoples become Christian fastest when least change of race or clan is involved." This recognition served as one of the key building blocks for the church growth movement that chose to adopt the HUP as a strategic insight rather than a sinful human tendency. Newbigin was opposed to such methodologies, as noted above, and I likewise can see no biblical or theological reason that such a tendency toward segregation should be endorsed as strategic no matter how expedient or pragmatic the results.

fellowship and friendship. A very tangible way to see that happen in a local church, then, is to encourage members to invite people they don't yet know to come over for a Sunday afternoon lunch rather than choosing to invite their old friends.

More than just a shared meal, those settings will provide rich opportunities to hear about the lives and experiences of people whose history and present situation may be different from yours. The act of listening well to one another will expose us to ways that perhaps our setting has shaped our priorities, perspectives, and preferences differently than for others. By understanding the perspective of another, we become aware of opportunities to intentionally defer to others' preferences, see the world through their eyes, and identify assumptions we might be making about church, discipleship, and fellowship that actually reinforce cultural barriers rather than crossing them.

Look Past the Clutter: Appealing to the Right Resources

Today in the American church there are loud voices shouting opinions in both support and rejection of various sociological theories and movements related to race and ethnicity. How church leaders respond to and receive the proposals of CRT and other theories has been at the center of recent evangelical firestorms. But what I hope has been accomplished in this chapter is to demonstrate that the church is uniquely equipped with our own resources for dealing with racial tensions that offer both a deeper explanation of their origins and a more robust solution for reconciliation. It begins with acknowledging the pervasiveness of sin and its effects on all relationships and perspectives.

Again, Newbigin is helpful as he reminds us of this astounding reality of the Christian message: one gospel creates one people out of those who have repeatedly and egregiously sinned against God and one another. He does not ignore the history of interpersonal sin nor the ongoing propensity to offend against one another in calling for unity. Instead, he argues that the resources available for healing and forgiveness are found in the single story of Scriptures that Christians—in all of our diversity—are called to inhabit. In his book *The Gospel in a Pluralist Society*, Newbigin puts it this way:

> Because we are always driven by our selfish desires and interests we will be aware that we require constant correction and that for this we must look to those who share the life in Christ but inhabit different cultural situations. We must always be ready to recognize that we have misrepresented the intention of Jesus because of our own interests. But that correction comes not from some supposed position of epistemological privilege outside the Christian story; it comes from the story itself when we expose ourselves honestly to the need of all people.[12]

---

12. Lesslie Newbigin, *The Gospel in a Pluralist Society* (Grand Rapids: Eerdmans, 1989), 151–52.

This point cuts to the heart of many of the contemporary discussions regarding the supposed epistemological privilege that grants special access to truth uniquely to different groups. While we should reject any proposal that privileges a certain group of people with truth that is inaccessible to others, this posture need not exempt us from expressing an empathetic desire to hear and understand our neighbor's point of view. It also recognizes there is no community that is not in need of subjecting their own sinful inclinations and perspectives to the clarifying call of biblical repentance and forgiveness.

As those who are still prone to sin and who are seeking to clearly see the world as it is despite sin-stained perceptions of it, our hope for epistemological certainty can come from no one group's perspective. Rather, our clarity concerning truth and how to live in its light must come as we willingly submit to Scripture's reshaping of all of our perspectives. In the context of relationships forged around a shared gospel identity, we find confidence to confront and to be confronted by brothers and sisters in ways that lead to meaningful repentance and reconciliation.

To that end, some diagnostic questions might be helpful to guide our assessment of the current state of our ministries. The following examples are intended to serve as fodder for prompting reflection within leadership teams, small groups, and personal relationships.

- Does your leadership team intentionality reflect and minister to the whole church?

- Is there a diversity of church members involved in assessing church ministries?
- Where are you engaged in conversations with believers from other cultures?
- Are you willing both to have your cultural blinders confronted and to confront others while you sit together under the authority of the Word?

These questions can begin to help a church in its structures, sermons, leaders, and relationships to manifest the gospel-centered unity that will adorn the gospel in compelling ways.

Newbigin envisions sinners and those sinned against coming together under the Scriptures as the setting most likely to produce meaningful reconciliation. As we do, the story of Scripture will convict offenders, draw out repentance, invite forgiveness, and reshape our shared approach to living as God's people together. He states it this way:

> Of course it is always required of us that we listen sensitively to both the desires and the needs of people, and that we try to understand their situation. But neither these desires and needs, nor any analysis of the situation made on the basis of some principles drawn from other sources than Scripture, can be the starting point for mission.

The starting point is God's revelation of himself
as it is witnessed to us in Scripture.[13]

Much like Paul confronting Peter for his gospel-obscuring
withdrawal from table fellowship with Gentiles in Galatians 2, the
Scriptures will challenge ways that we have practically separated
ourselves from our true unity. Conversations in which we seek to
understand the world through the eyes of our brothers and sisters
from different backgrounds will help all of us to identify ways
that we can develop more sensitivity to serving one another and
avoiding offense.

Reconciled and Reconciling in the Dining Room

These discussions often feel like a powder keg ready for
one poorly constructed sentence to spark an explosion. But
Newbigin has provided some helpful encouragement that these
conversations—tense as they can be—are worthy to be had. As
he looks at Jesus's ministry, Newbigin challenges us to avoid being
satisfied with ministering to a homogeneous subsection of society.
While Jesus came to Israel as a Jewish Messiah, his interactions
and ministry proved over and over his universal invitation to reconciliation with God. Newbigin highlights this diverse ministry
as he notes,

> If we turn to the ministry of Jesus himself, it is
> of course clear that Jesus shocked the established

---

13. Newbigin, *The Gospel in a Pluralist Society*, 153–54.

> authorities by being a friend to all—not only to the destitute and hungry, but also to those rich extortioners, the tax-collectors, whom all decent people ostracized; the shocking thing was not that he sided with the poor against the rich but that he met everyone equally with the same unlimited mercy and the same unconditioned demand for total loyalty.[14]

If the ministry of our Lord and Savior was not bound by social divisions, those ministering in his name must follow suit. As we do, we manifest the unity that we believe to be ultimately true in Christ. We also demonstrate the power of the gospel to a world that sees the effects of sin in current racial tensions, but which otherwise has no trustworthy resources or hope to resolve it.

By donning our missionary lenses, we see that churches have a vital role to play in providing examples of reconciliation across otherwise divided demographics. Working to live out a diverse unity is both a proper result of our theological convictions and is a display of the power of the gospel to a watching world. As we engage the conversation about race and ethnicity as Christians, we do so with the gospel-centered resources needed to produce recognition of sin, prejudice, and injustice at the same time as offering the hope of repentance, forgiveness, and reconciliation.

As we close this chapter, it needs to be said again that I do not believe these church-centered recommendations suffice to address

---

14. Newbigin, *The Gospel in a Pluralist Society*, 151.

all of the problems in the US. Neither do I intend to side-step the real and important discussions that need to take place more broadly and on a national level. I do not offer these initial recommendations as if they provide an easy solution to what are weighty and complicated historical problems that have knotty contemporary ramifications. Nor do I want to communicate there is no role for some pastors and particular congregations to be directly involved in some of these broader discussions. These conversations simply deserve more attention and expertise than space allows in a chapter like this.

What I do intend to point our attention to is that a local congregation can begin addressing the real problems existing in their communities due to tensions between different ethnicities and cultures by using the resources available to us in the gospel, in Scripture, and through fellowship. After all, we cannot hope to have our neighbors listen to our advice if we have not gotten our own house in order.

Chapter 4

Our Living Room

Theology Divorced from Real Life

Once we had a plan for removing some of the clutter in the dining room, it was on to the living room. This space had hosted countless family movie nights, play dates with friends, and holiday celebrations with extended family. It was the space we went to at the end of the day after we had kicked off our shoes. Its tattered furniture had caught our exhausted bodies on many occasions as we collapsed after a hard day's work or a late-night backyard basketball game. In some ways, this room represented respite for the family—a place of rest and a place where we let our hair down with one another.

But as I looked at the room from the perspective of a potential buyer, I noticed for the first time a strange feature of this inner sanctum of the Bennett home: there were no window treatments. One wall facing the neighbor's house was nearly all windows, and the wall facing the street was likewise predominantly composed of glass. While this design welcomed generous amounts of natural light, it also reduced our privacy.

I thought back to times when my sisters and I had been in this room watching episodes of *Walker, Texas Ranger*—a TV series starring Chuck Norris as a law enforcement agent who was a martial arts master. During commercial breaks we would test our karate skills on one another, trying to imitate Norris as he defeated bad guys with no remorse. Little had we considered that the windows put our pathetic kicks, off-kilter spins, and wimpy punches on full display for onlookers.

As I reflected on how visible our private family moments were to strangers who happened to glance through the windows, it made me realize just how exposed this room was. We let our hair—and our guard—down in that room. We behaved according to the perception of privacy. It made me wonder how many of our private moments we had unknowingly shared with outsiders.

> **The American church is increasingly visible to those looking in from the outside.**

How many embarrassing things did the neighbors see us doing? How many hours did they note my sisters and me dedicating to video games and movies? How many tense family disagreements did they accidentally eavesdrop on? And, having seen all of that, what impression did they have about who we really were as a family?

Just like this living room, the American church is increasingly visible to those looking in from the outside. It is important to consider whether what they see when our hair is down corresponds to what they hear when we preach the gospel of Jesus in our Sunday best.

The Gospel: Faith That Works

When Lesslie Newbigin discussed the gospel, he had in mind an all-encompassing reality. For Newbigin, the essence of the gospel could not be divorced from its effects. The essence of the gospel, as defined by Paul in 1 Corinthians 15, is a message of God's faithful, sin-defeating work on behalf of sinners through the life, death, and resurrection of Jesus. But the effects of this gospel are manifold and manifest in a community of gospel-changed lives. It was important for Newbigin—as it was for Paul and as it is for us today—that the gospel effects emerge from the essence without supplanting it.

During Newbigin's time, many of his coworkers began to conflate the effects of the gospel with the gospel itself. They argued that things like creation care, economic equality, and social justice issues were part of the essence of the gospel. Newbigin resisted such a conflation, while yet maintaining a robust understanding of the gospel's claim on human lives. He recognized first and foremost the gospel was a message to be received in faith of God's faithfulness in Christ to atone for sins. To this point, Newbigin writes,

> [The gospel is] a factual statement. Namely, that
> at a certain point in history, the history of this

world, God who is the author, the sustainer, the
goal of all that exists, of all being and all meaning
and all truth, has become present in our human
history as the man Jesus, who we can know and
who we can love and serve; and that by His incar-
nation, His ministry, His death and resurrection,
He has finally broken the powers that oppress us
and has created a space and a time in which we
who are unholy can nevertheless live in fellowship with a God who is holy.[1]

However, he also recognized it was a transforming story into
which believers were assumed. For Newbigin, the divide between
believing the gospel and living as those transformed by the gospel
was artificial.

In the midst of rejecting such a dichotomy, Newbigin notes
the tendency within Christian debates to artificially divide
between faith and action, and between the gospel and its effects.
In an address entitled *Church, World, Kingdom*, Newbigin writes:

The story of missions, from the days of Henry
Martyn until now, is also punctuated with fierce
internal debates about the propriety or otherwise
of this massive involvement in social, economic,
and political affairs. . . . [I am referring to] the

---

1. Lesslie Newbigin, "Church, World, Kingdom," 95–109 in *Signs Amid
the Rubble: The Purposes of God in Human History*, ed. Geoffrey Wainwright
(Grand Rapids: Eerdmans, 2003), 113.

internal debate among Christians about the large role of educational, medical, and socio-economic programs in the work of missions over the past two centuries. Over and over again the complaint is made that these have crowded the one essential—namely, explicit evangelism. The powerful Church Growth school has this as one of its main contentions. Over and over again in missionary history, new bodies have been founded with the avowed intention of concentrating on pure evangelism, and over and over again they have in turn been drawn into other activities of the kind I have referred to. And indeed it is the very nature of the gospel itself which always defeats these attempts to separate the word from the deed, to give one primacy over the other, because the gospel is precisely good news of the Word made flesh.[2]

Having served as a theologically conservative and evangelistically minded member of the World Council of Churches and the International Missionary Council, Newbigin recognized the two poles of social activism and mere proclamation as twin dangers that perennially face the Christian. Yet he refused to choose one ditch over the other. He wanted the life Christians lived to be transformed by the gospel story they proclaimed.

---

2. Lesslie Newbigin, "Church, World, Kingdom," 98–99.

In one of his most popular works, *The Gospel in a Pluralist Society*, Newbigin writes of his desire that theology be derived from a common source (biblical truth) and toward an embodied life (biblical action). He writes,

> I am thus again stressing the priority of the gospel as the message, embodied in an actual story, of what God has in fact done, is doing, and will do. Christian theology is a form of rational discourse developed within the community which accepts the primacy of this story and seeks actively to live in the world in accordance with the story.[3]

Later in the same book, Newbigin clarifies that evangelism and action must go together within the story told in Scripture, writing, "Evangelism that is politically and ideologically naïve, and social action which does not recognize the need for conversion from false gods to the living God, both fall short of what is required."[4]

While this expectation that the church must live out the story it believes is most readily connected to Christian growth and sanctification, Newbigin is keen to point out its missiological role. As the church lives out a better and all-encompassing story, it naturally confronts the stories told by onlookers. If it is beautiful and holistic, it lends credibility to the Christian claim that the biblical

---

3. Lesslie Newbigin, *The Gospel in a Pluralist Society* (Grand Rapids: Eerdmans, 1989), 152.

4. Newbigin, *The Gospel in a Pluralist Society*, 210.

story is the one true story of the universe. We saw this play out on the mission field firsthand.

Missionary Community: Proclamation and Demonstration

In 2012 our missionary team of five people was preparing to move to North Africa, where it is illegal to be a Christian missionary. We would be required to find a way to access the country and remain there legally and on our own. In recognizing our dependence upon the Lord for discerning a wise means of accessing the country, our team took a weekend away, committed to fasting and praying, and then came together to discuss a path forward. As we considered how we would gain and retain access to the country, we determined that whatever direction we went, our solution must address three central questions: (a) What can we do that will naturally connect us to the people we are trying to share the gospel with? (b) What can we do that will allow us to involve people from our sending churches in meaningful ministry along the way? And (c) What can we do with excellence so the beauty and truth of the gospel we proclaim is reinforced by the lives we live and the work we do?

Having entertained a number of different possibilities, our team came back to a time-tested means of creative access: we taught English as a Second Language. We had been certified by reputable ESL programs, and as native English speakers we were viewed by the culture as a commodity. We would be able to connect short-term visitors from our home churches with English speaking nationals without having to rely on translators. This was not a flashy, cutting-edge strategy, but it met the criteria that we had prayerfully determined our access point required.

Being foreign business owners in a place with reason to be suspicious of outsiders, we needed to ensure our business was run according to all of the country's legal standards. The suspicion of outsiders also meant we could expect some of our students would likely be serving as informants for secret police. We needed to make sure our operations were totally above board, and that meant we could not use our business for overt evangelism. As a result, we adopted a policy that in the classroom we would not speak about either politics or religion. We announced this policy at the beginning of each four-week semester, and we reinforced it when students started to veer in the direction of either of those topics while class was in session.

It may have seemed that this was an abdication of our central purpose for gaining access via an ESL business. But in the end, such clear prohibitions in the classroom became something of a joke for our students, and it also ignited their curiosity about what we thought when topics of political or religious interest would arise. As soon as we left the premises with groups of students heading to local coffee shops after class, they would pepper us with the questions they were not allowed to ask in class. This provided much more fruitful engagement, as it was student-driven and it allowed for those sensitive discussions to occur in more personal settings.

But the thing that was more important for our purposes here was how the students observed our teaching as evidence of genuine concern for them. As we became more established in the community, we developed a reputation of being excellent English teachers who actually wanted their clients to succeed. I heard a number of students who worked through our classrooms remark, "There is something so different about you all at this center. You actually care about us, seem to love one another, and are not the types of Americans we are used to seeing come through here on holiday."

For these national friends, the way we did our work in the classroom made sense in light of the God we explained to them in the cafes. They were watching our lives—whether we knew it or not—and while we were certainly imperfect and inconsistent in our display of gospel-shaped living, many saw in us a genuine kind of transformed living that provided an embodied example of the gospel we proclaimed.

To be clear, as these friends and neighbors saw us as a different breed of Americans, they had not yet encountered the essence of the gospel. As noted above, the gospel is not transformed lives, but it is the proclamation that the incarnate, crucified, resurrected, and ascended Son of God has satisfied God's wrath against sin and extended atonement through faith to all who will believe. Being a caring teacher who demonstrates a notable excellence and care for students in the classroom is an effect of the gospel, but not a self-interpreting display of the message of Jesus's atoning work and royal reign.

Still, our convictions that emerge from the gospel drove our pursuit of excellence and our expressions of compassion. As onlookers asked why we were compassionate and dedicated to our teaching, we had opportunity to speak to the essence of the gospel that drove us to exhibit these external effects. And for others who had heard us proclaim the gospel, when they noticed the way we expressed genuine brotherly love for one another as a team and demonstrated neighborly concern for our students, they saw the validating fruits of the message we had claimed was central to our lives.

The same questions we asked about how to most strategically shape our creative access to the country could be asked by Christians at home. When helping youth determine their courses of study and vocational trajectories, we might ask them to consider how their gifts, skills, and passions might be well-suited to meet gospel-strategic needs. We might also encourage our people who are already connected to occupations that are often considered "secular" to reconceive of their office-hours as investments in ministry. And we might look around our community and ask, "Do our lives and ministries in this community exhibit a compassion and concern for the hurting, the broken, and the marginalized that would reinforce the message of gospel-transformation that we preach?"

Peering into Our Living Room

At this point, it is worth considering what an onlooker might see as they glance through the windows of the American church. Over the last few decades, the windows into the church have become far less opaque than the stained-glass windows of generations past, and far more transparent and easily seen through—like the windows into my family's living room. From social engagement to social media, the members that compose the church are being observed for how their truth claims affect life change.

The stories of those who have "deconstructed" their faith today are riddled with claims of intellectual dissatisfaction with the Christian faith. In the deconstruction stories I have observed, however, the stated reasons for leaving evangelicalism don't often seem to be the primary reason they are walking away. More often, those leaving evangelicalism relate stories of hearing certain dogmas championed—love, grace, mercy, kindness—but then watching or experiencing the effects of members of the church publicly exhibit the opposite qualities.[5]

Many onlookers—both those who have never been part of the faith and those who have left it—watch church folk and ministry leaders who claim to be pro-life protesting the placement of Afghani immigrants in their community. They watch those who say, "Love the sinner, hate the sin," hold sinners at arm's length until they are clean enough to associate with them. And they watch people—whose Lord took on the form of a servant to rescue sinners—step on their peers as they clamor selfishly for the top positions at work. That there are plenty of examples of

---

5. I commend to you the various chapters of the helpful book edited by, Ivan Mesa, *Before You Lose Your Faith: Deconstructing Doubt in the Church* (Austin, TX: TGC, 2021). The brief chapters unveil different types of experiential dissatisfaction with expressions of the Christian faith that claim to produce a compassionate and compelling life but which often are observed as stale, irrelevant, and calloused.

this irreconcilable faith-life dichotomy is a true shame upon those who claim the gospel.

As a shepherd of the flock entrusted to him, Paul charged Timothy in 1 Timothy 4:16 to be sure to keep a close watch on both his life and his teaching. So too will a church entrusted with being a signpost of the kingdom for a lost world have a missiological reason to keep a close watch on both its doctrine and its display. If we are to truly communicate the good news of life under King Jesus's rule to a skeptical world, we will need to be show-and-tell churches.

Faith and Works

Just like the churches of Newbigin's day, contemporary evangelicalism is divided over whether the church should prioritize gospel proclamation or demonstration. Should the church be primarily concerned with teaching doctrine or embodying it? Should we focus on being a people known for how the Bible informs our beliefs or how our beliefs transform our lives? Is it more important to articulate the content of our faith or that our faith speaks through our actions? This is one area where a missionary's lenses can help to clarify a muddied American conversation.

A missionary enters a culture with a commitment to the truth and a compassion for the lost. The purpose that drives them to a context is to see the gospel proclaimed, believed, and transforming the people who currently are caught in idolatry. That overarching motivation saturates a missionary's vision for how they represent themselves in every moment of the day because of the awareness that they are always representing the message they proclaim.

Newbigin calls this process, "learning to live by the true story."[6] All throughout his writings, Newbigin is keen to call not just individuals but whole churches to teach and preach the true story and then to live it out as a signpost of the kingdom. In one place he states it this way:

> The business of [the church] is to be an effective sign, instrument, and firstfruit of God's purpose for the whole city. Each of those three words is important. They are to be a *sign*, pointing men to something that is beyond their present horizon but can give guidance and hope now; an *instrument* (but not the only one) that God can use for his work of healing, liberating, and blessing; and a *firstfruit*—a place where men and women can have a real taste now of the joy and freedom God intends for us all.[7]

One of the aspects of being a sign that Newbigin highlights is active evangelism within the context of caring community engagement. He puts it this way, "Anyone who has a faith that he really believes . . . wants to persuade others to believe it too. If you do not want to share it with others, it is not your real faith.

------

6. Lesslie Newbigin, *A Word in Season: Perspectives in Christian World Missions* (Grand Rapids: Eerdmans, 1994), 204.

7. Newbigin, *A Word in Season*, 33.

But—and this is a big 'but'—no one is going to listen to your evangelism unless he sees that it comes out of a fellowship that cares."[8] And lest a reader think his efforts dissolve into a bland and gospel-less charity, Newbigin praises one of his coworkers as he describes his response to a non-Christian in the context of a community sanitation project:

> While we were engaged in the public sanitation program one of our workers was asked, "What are you doing this for? Are you trying to convert us?" It would have been easy for him to answer, "Oh no, we are just trying to help you." To say that would have meant that we were not taking the people seriously. He answered, "Of course we are trying to convert you; do you think we want to leave you as you are?"[9]

Newbigin can champion this radically changed life that is eager to see others' lives changed as well because of his more holistic expectation of the effects of conversion, which he defines as "being so changed that you become an agent of change."[10] Taking people seriously requires that we treat them as embodied souls who both need a rescue from sin and a rescue from sin's effects.

One of the problems we face in this discussion is that we have biased our language by using binary labels. Historically, those

---

8. Newbigin, *A Word in Season*, 34.

9. Newbigin, *A Word in Season*, 37.

10. Newbigin, *A Word in Season*, 37.

who have prioritized proclamation and doctrine have been labeled conservatives or fundamentalists. In contemporary discussions such groups are keen to advocate for precision regarding the articulation of atonement, biblical inerrancy, human sexuality, the roles of men and women in the church and in the home, and other important issues that influence today's social landscape. These are all important topics, and it is right to argue for biblically informed positions on these issues in a world that lacks a sturdy foundation for its varied conclusions.

On the other hand, those who see gospel-driven action to be most necessary as a demonstration of gospel hope and beauty tend to be labeled as progressives or liberals. Supporting impoverished communities, caring for orphans, single mothers, and refugees, and advocating for the underrepresented in society tend to be the significant topics of concern for people inclined toward gospel-driven action. Again, there is good biblical warrant for much of this advocacy. Likewise, engagement in these broader civic concerns allows believers to demonstrate the gospel-driven compassion that seeks to address brokenness and injustice.

> **Taking people seriously requires that we treat them as embodied souls who both need a rescue from sin and a rescue from sin's effects.**

The problems with these binary divisions and dualistic designations are manifold. First, *they use language that is freighted in our day with political baggage.* "Conservative" and "liberal"—while technically descriptive of the tendencies they are identifying—are words used to describe the secular political spectrum and representative approaches to similar issues. In American evangelical Christianity, the use of such language reinforces an inappropriate conflation of two separate arenas of theology and politics. And unfortunately, for many American Christians, their political allegiances often threaten to precede their gospel-analysis of issues at hand.

This works itself out when a church or a pastor begins to speak about how to care for the poor or refugees in the community. It won't be long before someone grumbles that the pastor is a liberal or a Marxist. Or, on the other hand, if a pastor or church teaches a historic biblical sexual ethic, they will be labeled as fundamentalist conservatives or misogynists. In reality, these issues are not incompatible with one another, and both are derived from biblical teaching. But for fear of being labeled by either side, sometimes churches and pastors are reticent to engage in either the care for the vulnerable in a community or the convictional teaching of biblical norms.

Second, *the labels reinforce the false assumption that one can be either a belief-focused Christian or an action-focused Christian.* The reality is that Christians are not at liberty to choose between one or the other. Belief and action go together.

The call to the gospel is a call to believe an objective message about Jesus as the king of the universe. It is not *merely* a means to making a more compassionate society. At the same time, Jesus's kingdom calls for more than *merely* assenting to his reign. King Jesus demands a total submission of one's life and a reorienting of one's priorities as a member of the kingdom. To pretend that one of these issues can eclipse the other is a false dilemma that has caused both sides to defend their indefensible attempts to divide that which God has delivered together.

The American church would do well, then, to stop allowing the false binary of these labels to sever the biblical connection between the essence of the gospel and the effects of the gospel. Rather than fearing association with a given label or party, we need to break free of the false idea that those who care for the marginalized automatically do so at risk of losing the gospel message. And we must also dissuade ourselves of the idea that if we teach the exclusive message of salvation in Christ and life according to a biblical ethic that we are somehow at risk of being less-than-loving. The watching world needs to see and hear the message we have to show and tell them. And when our faith moves us into action of conviction and compassion, the King and his kingdom issue a compelling and holistic call to the gospel.

Clarity and Charity

Before concluding this chapter, I want to point out one more contemporary way the world is peering into the church's living room: social media. The way that we portray ourselves on social media often exposes two more poles that tear apart the integrity of our message: *theological clarity and interpersonal charity.*

On the one hand, Jesus prayed that his followers would be united in his gospel and that their love for one another would be a visible apologetic for the message they proclaimed. If we are to live out that prayer, we must be committed to living united to one another in the gospel that we share.

On the other hand, Scripture calls on believers to contend for the faith once delivered to all the saints. It is therefore incumbent upon believers to identify false teaching within the church. We cannot abide gospel-denying claims in hopes that our display of community will suffice as an apologetic.

Unfortunately, we are all-too-quick to tear into one another for failing to achieve what we perceive to be appropriate nuance in a 140-character statement on Twitter. For many reasons, I am cautious and somewhat critical of Facebook, Twitter, and other similar social media platforms. Still, I recognize they can provide many opportunities to discover helpful resources, insightful perspectives, and contemporary discussions both within the church and without. For that reason, I am not ready to throw social media out completely.

However, I have grieved deeply over the lack of charity exhibited by many of my brothers and sisters as they have dunked on one another and undermined confidence in one another's orthodoxy in order to get likes and retweets. I have literally wept as I have read the book of Acts against the backdrop of scathing Twitter coverage of the recent convention meetings of several large denominations.

One example of this heart-wrenching juxtaposition between the early church and contemporary American evangelicalism can be seen in Acts 4:32, which states, "Now the entire group of those who believed were of one heart and mind, and no one claimed that any of his possessions was his own, but instead they held everything in common." In ugly contrast to this, I have seen brothers and sisters on social media call into question the faith of other brothers and sisters because of their willingness to engage in discussions that are assumed to align them with a particular political party.

We do well to remember even in our social media activity the world is watching. When we defame one another to make a name for ourselves, or when we respond without the charity fitting for gospel-siblings to extend to one another, we often undermine our witness in the eyes of the world. When we give the world reasons to question the integrity of our gospel-born relationships, we also give the world reasons to doubt the integrity of our gospel message.

The Compelling Community of Living Faith

The American church has its living room windows wide open in ways that allow the world to look in at most of what goes on inside. This chapter has uncovered some ways we may be failing to connect the essence of the gospel with the effects it should be having in our lives, ministries, and relationships. Newbigin has reminded us that the church is to be a display of the gospel in its proclaimed faith and its embodied living.

Putting on our missionary lenses, then, we see that when we maintain an artificial division between faith and action, we risk undermining the gospel by either speaking of its transforming power while refusing to live transformed lives or by living out compassion while not basing that compassion upon the objective message of the gospel. On the other hand, when we both proclaim the gospel of King Jesus and live as those who serve his kingdom agenda, the truth and integrity of the gospel are put on compelling display.

As we conclude this chapter in search of practical application, it is helpful to again consult Lesslie Newbigin. In *The Gospel in a Pluralist Society,* Newbigin lists six aspects of churches that are poised to display Jesus's character to the watching world and to one another. These six aspects have both corporate and individual application and can serve as a good way of assessing where we might need to grow to better live out the gospel we hold out.

As Newbigin begins defining the gospel-transformed community of the church, he notes first that *the church must be a community primarily centered on praise and worship of God,* whose incarnate and costly redemption has made way for a new humanity in Christ. Second, *it must be a community of truth drawn from the pages of Scripture* as the revealed truth from the author of truth. Third, *it must be a community of people that refuses to exist merely for itself* but will be deeply involved in the concerns of its context. As Newbigin often states, a local church is not just a church *in* a place, but it is also the church *for* a place. That requires a church to consider how its gospel message will call its gospel-changed people to work toward effecting gospel-driven change by addressing the needs of the community around it.

As Newbigin continues his list, his fourth element of a transformed and community-transforming church is perhaps most pertinent in my mind. Newbigin urges churches to be communities wherein *men and women are prepared for and encouraged in the task of serving as priests and ministers for the world.* Connected to this, the fifth characteristic is that *this community will be marked by a real sense of mutual responsibility.* Each one will recognize that they must—as parts of a body—exercise their gifts of ministry in order to function collectively in the task of being an embassy of Christ's kingdom on earth. And sixth, Newbigin recognizes that *in the midst of a hopeless and bleak world, the church of Jesus the risen and returning Lord must be a community of hope.*[11]

It is noteworthy to consider that our team in North Africa was never accused of neglecting gospel proclamation because of our investment in teaching English. On the mission field, and in places where creative access is required, onlookers are more willing to see how ministry is actually amplified through teaching, medical care, mercy ministries, and other gospel-driven engagements. Why would we think it might be otherwise at home?

Rather than thinking the so-called secular vocations of church members are extraneous to their lives as gospel-changed people, what if we regularly pointed out that our occupations serve as great conduits for gospel-proclamation? What if churches regularly called their people to be excellent employees and citizens as a natural expression of their transformed hearts and as a testimony to their convictions? What would happen if we intentionally started thinking with seniors in high school about how they might choose their career paths using some of the strategic questions our North Africa team asked? While churches in America do not have

---

11. These six points are drawn from Newbigin, *The Gospel in a Pluralist Society*, 227–33.

the same concerns regarding their legal right to exist, what would happen if we taught our people to ask the same sorts of missiologically strategic questions about their employment and civic involvement? And what if we committed to engaging with one another in ways that press toward clarity and biblically solid theology while also defaulting toward charity and mutual respect?

> **What if we regularly pointed out that our occupations serve as great conduits for gospel-proclamation?**

Transformed lives are not the gospel, but they do provide an apologetic for the gospel. Brotherly love and neighborly compassion are not the gospel, but the living gospel produces such things in those who have repented, believed, and been called to start living the resurrection life of those in Christ. Our convictions and our compassion are not to be separated from one another. And when they work together, they provide a compelling apologetic for the gospel.

As we consider how our family presents itself to a world looking in through our living room windows, it is right for us to revisit Newbigin's charge to us to be both the proclaimers and imitators of King Jesus:

> Authentic Christian thought and action . . . must begin and continue by attending to what God has done in the story of Israel and supremely in the story of Jesus Christ. It must continue by indwelling that story so that it is our story, the

way we understand the real story. And then, and this is the vital point, to attend with open hearts and minds to the real needs of people in the way that Jesus attended to them, knowing that the real need is that which can only be satisfied by everything that comes from the mouth of God (Matt. 4:4). As we share in the life and worship of the Church, through fellowship, word, and sacrament, we indwell the story and from within that story we seek to be the voice and the hands of Jesus for our time and place.[12]

May we learn to so indwell the gospel story that our lives would display both our commitment to the truth and the beautiful community it produces, for one another and in front of a watching world.

---

12. Newbigin, *The Gospel in a Pluralist Society*, 151.

Chapter 5

Our Bedroom

Sexual Idolatry in the Sanctuary

Heading up to the second floor, we needed to clear out the bedrooms to stage them for the realtor. Standing in the doorway of the room my parents had always slept in, I had a wave of claustrophobia settle over me. Jam-packed into the space was a suffocating collection of furniture that would need to be cleared out to show off the room to prospective buyers. A massive dresser with a vanity mirror covered one wall, a cluttered computer desk was tucked into the far corner, and a chest of drawers stood immediately to the right of the doorway.

Most of the room, however, was taken up by the gigantic waterbed that my parents had slept in for as long as I could remember. The already oversized bed was encased in a heavy wooden frame with a tall, mirrored headboard. The mass of its frame added to its dimensions, consuming two-thirds of the room.

As I surveyed the room, I was reminded of how difficult it always had been trying to navigate the tight space as an over-sized high schooler. I remembered having to squeeze sideways through the narrow passage between the edge of the bed and the chest of drawers, and then having to fold myself awkwardly into the computer chair—usually with a bruise shaped like the corner of the bedframe forming on my calf or my thigh. The bed just took up so much space that it could not be avoided, imposing itself upon what felt like every square inch of the room.

Being on the second floor, I wondered about how we were going to dismantle this gigantic eyesore in order to bring a more reasonably sized bed in for the staging. Draining the bed, disassembling it, and then hauling it outside for rubbish removal was half a day's effort. But in the end, the room looked much more spacious and appropriately apportioned when we had done so. We brought up an old bedframe and queen-sized mattress from the basement, and when it was assembled, it fit much more comfortably, making it feel as if the room had doubled in size.

I couldn't help but note the difference between the way the first bed fit in this space and the way the table stood at the center of the dining room. Where the dining room table seemed to expand the room, the waterbed had completely consumed the space.

The American Bedroom: A Shrine to Sexual Idolatry

The overwhelming size of the waterbed in my parents' bedroom is analogous to the way that sex occupies a suffocatingly outsized role in American culture. Of course, sex and sexuality are certainly important aspects of human life. But in American culture they have come to dominate and drive everything. From the way we entertain ourselves to the way we identify ourselves, sex and sexuality are front and center everywhere we look. It is no secret that American society is obsessed with sex.

For decades, marketers and advertisers have capitalized on our sex-obsession by linking their products with promises of sexual fulfillment. In so doing, they are attempting to tap into the deeper motivations they perceive to be driving their customers—motivations that transcend mere desire for transportation and breath-freshening. Given the sexualization of everything from cars to candies, it would seem as though sex is the core motivator in America.

> **Sex occupies a suffocatingly outsized role in American culture.**

Many Americans have fashioned sex into a god and given their lives over to its service in hopes it will provide ultimate fulfillment. The Bible gives us language to identify those deep-seated hopes and desires that we pursue feverishly in an insatiable search for ultimate satisfaction: idolatry.

But in recent years, sex—and the related conversation of gender—has transcended mere pleasure seeking and taken on the role of defining individuals. Our culture has begun looking to sex and gender as more than preferences. Now, sex provides custom-fit identities. If an individual deems it appropriate, they may decouple their biological sex from their self-determined gender identity to better describe who they most truly understand them-selves to be. Sex has now been made to carry the weight of our ultimate hopes and our ultimate meaning.

While sexual promiscuity and sexual identity might at first seem unrelated, I believe a missionary lens will help us to see the two as intertwined. We see this most clearly when we consider that both are expressions of a more fundamental assertion of the ultimate importance of the individual. Though we might notice examples of the idolatry of the individual most readily in the sur-rounding culture, we will come to see this is not merely a problem outside of the church.

Even though the American evangelicalism has largely resisted the dissolution of sexual and gender boundaries, the American church has not always adequately irradicated the underlying idolatry of sex and individualism. Appealing to biblical ethics, we have regulated some of the expressions of sex. Likewise, we have typically upheld the importance of the givenness of one's identity. But we have not always addressed the underlying idolatries that have driven the culture to excess and extremes.

To use biblical imagery, we have not always torn down the Asherah poles: we have sometimes simply placed moral fences around them.

If the cultural perspective on sex is a problem of idolatry, then the solution must be more than mere moralism. The solu-tion must supplant the central role that sexual gratification and individual self-determination play in our society. It must redirect our attention to God as the one with the exclusive right to our worship. We must reclaim the biblical story in which sex has a place, but not at the center.

Identifying Idolatry through Missionary Lenses

When Newbigin ministered in India, it was commonplace for him to pass by Hindu temples filled with idols and to encounter graven images in household shrines when visiting his neighbors. These idols were easily identified by their physical presence and by the attention drawn to them when worshippers prostrated before them or presented them with gifts.

When he returned to England with eyes accustomed to seeing idol worship, Newbigin found fewer temples than he had seen in India, but still detected evidence of rampant idolatry. He wrote incisively about the Western idolatry of individualism, materialism, and secularism. Yet he was not satisfied to merely observe that the secular West was just as idolatrous as its Indian neighbors. He issued a call to battle.

Six years prior to his death, Newbigin urged his readers to see, "The 'secular' society is not a neutral area into which we can project the Christian message. It is an area already occupied by other gods. We have a battle on our hands. We are dealing with principalities and powers."[1] This summons is woven throughout all of Newbigin's writing as he reminds us that the biblical story

---

1. Lesslie Newbigin, "Evangelism in the Context of Secularization," 148–57 in *A Word in Season: Perspectives in Christian World Missions* (Grand Rapids: Eerdmans, 1994), 150.

will not accommodate itself to rivals—it supplants and confronts all alternatives.

While Newbigin's identification of Western idolatries focuses on materialism and individualism more extensively than issues of sex, sexuality does not escape the implications of his insight. In fact, as we assess the current American house, it is worth drawing out two specific places where Newbigin's contributions confront us today: sexual idolatry and sexual identity.

Sexual Idolatry

As noted above, in Newbigin's return to the "secular" West he found the Western worldview was no less religious than the idol-saturated environment he had left behind in India. In an essay entitled, "Evangelism in the Context of Secularization," Newbigin notes insightfully, "It is clear that there are, even in the most secularized societies, forces that have a religious character in the sense that they have the status of dogma and command total trust."[2]

He goes on to observe that when we jettison the "superstitions" of religion in favor of scientific

> When we jettison the "superstitions" of religion in favor of scientific explanations of *how* the world works, we forfeit the opportunity to answer the *why* questions that divine revelation alone can provide.

2. Newbigin, "Evangelism in the Context of Secularization," 149.

explanations of *how* the world works, we forfeit the opportunity to answer the *why* questions that divine revelation alone can provide. Such an omission creates a vacuum into which humans naturally and inevitably assume all sorts of distractions. He writes,

> In the end, the society we have is not a secular society but a pagan society, a society in which men and women are giving their allegiance to no-gods. The rational part of us puts its trust in the findings of science but is left with no answer to the question of ultimate meaning. The way is open for the irrational part of us to develop a pantheon of idols.[3]

Much like the European culture Newbigin encountered, the American cultural landscape is dotted with shrines to multiple idols. Chief among them is sexual gratification and expression.

Lest we think the church is free of the impact of this idolatry, however, we must consider whether we have smuggled these idols into our sanctuaries. We will look at ways the American church can benefit from donning the idol-detecting lenses of Newbigin later in this chapter. Before doing so, however, we need to look at a second aspect of Newbigin's insight related to our contemporary culture's focus on sex. The second area that Newbigin's insight comes to bear on our inspection of the American bedroom is at the point of individually determined sexual or gender identity.

---

3. Newbigin, "Evangelism in the Context of Secularization," 150.

Sexual Identity

One of the most cherished values in America is the individual right to assert and to define oneself. We love and promote the idea of self-making. Yet Newbigin's time in a collectivist culture prepared him to recognize ways that the hyper-individualism of the West can be detrimental to the social and communal aspects of human existence.

The rugged individualism prized by American values reinforces the false idea that individuals are the center of their own stories. We believe ourselves free to determine every aspect of who we will be, including our sexuality and gender. Newbigin takes aim at this confidence of the individual to both know themselves and construct their identity:

> The error is the supposition that it is we who are the explorers, that the real questions are the ones we formulate and put to the universe, and that our minds have a sovereign freedom to explore a reality waiting to be discovered. Our peril is that, out of the vastness of the unplumbed mystery, we summon up images that are the creations of our own minds. The human heart, as Calvin said, is a factory of idols.[4]

Newbigin goes on to critique the idea that an unaided individual is capable of not only exploring but also rightly perceiving

---

4. Lesslie Newbigin, *Proper Confidence: Faith, Doubt, and Certainty in Christian Discipleship* (Grand Rapids: Eerdmans, 1995), 104.

the world as it is. He points to the folly of making ourselves the center of the universe, writing,

> [The gospel] exposes as illusion the . . . picture of ourselves as sovereign explorers who formulate the real questions in a search for a yet-to-be-discovered reality. The gospel undermines our questions with a question that comes to us from the mystery we thought to explore. . . . We are *not* honest and open-minded explorers of reality; we are alienated from reality because we have made ourselves the center of the universe.[5]

Again, Newbigin did not here specifically engage the contemporary concept of sexual identity. However, he does dig under its foundations to inspect the individualistic assumptions that the development of a sexual identity rests upon.

These critiques applied to Newbigin's England, and they also apply to today's America. As we don our missionary lenses, we will also see some gospel-critical reasons for us to root out our own sexual idolatry and to hold out an identity that is far sturdier than anything that can be constructed around sexual activity.

Inspecting the Church with Missionary Lenses

As my wife and I returned to the US from having lived in the Middle East, we found ourselves freshly confronted with

---

5. Newbigin, *Proper Confidence*, 104.

the hyper-sexualized environment of America. Middle Eastern culture, saturated by Islamic influence, presents a wildly different approach to sex and sexuality than what one sees splashed brazenly across the billboards and sitcoms in the United States. Public discussion about sex remains taboo in the Middle East, and if a woman's ankles or hair are visible it is considered immodest.

Now, there are certainly many aspects of Middle Eastern approaches to sexuality that need to be critiqued and exposed as harmful. I certainly do not intend to endorse the often misogynistic and dehumanizing practices throughout the region that are marketed as modesty and propriety. Rather, I simply note this contrast between the culture we came from and the culture we found in our homecoming was jarring, and clearly reminded us that in America, sex is god.

Our initial experience with this reverse-culture shock came as we drove down the road and saw shameless billboards publicly advertising "gentlemen's" clubs and flaunting these shrines to sexuality at the next exit. The shock continued as we found discussions about sexual and gender identity permeating what seemed like every area of life, from bathrooms to schools.

Looking at both of these issues through missionary lenses, we began to see two gospel-centered issues at hand. First, *the introduction of the category of sexual identity or gender identity into our vocabulary challenges the church to uphold the biblical teaching about God's design for his creatures and his creation.* However, merely teaching a biblical vision of male and female does not sufficiently address the gospel-level need of those attempting to build something as weighty as an identity on a foundation as feeble as sex. If the church is to take a missionary posture toward those engaged in the futile process of self-making, we must go beyond simply defending the biblical sexual ethic. We must engage in ministry that taps into the deeper identity offered in Christ.

Second, I alluded to the fact that *the idolatry of sex mentioned above is not something that merely occurs outside of the church.* Having been trained to find ways that cultures naturally incline worship toward things that are not God, we might find ourselves catching glimpses of how the promises that drive secular culture toward sexual idolatry—satisfaction, ultimate fulfilment, joy, meaning—have seeped into the sanctuary unnoticed. We as Christians have, at times, allowed the promises of sexual gratification to be whispered unchallenged, while settling for merely regulating the *who, when,* and *how* of sex. Let's unpack these two areas a bit more.

> **We as Christians have, at times, allowed the promises of sexual gratification to be whispered unchallenged, while settling for merely regulating the *who, when,* and *how* of sex.**

Sexual Identity: An Insufficient Foundation

Having returned from the Middle East and reintegrated into the American church, we have found that the churches we have participated in are adept at defending a biblical sexual ethic against a ceaseless tide of secular attack. This defense is perennially necessary and good in contrast to the "you do you" approach to sexual preferences espoused by secular culture.

But if we don missionary glasses in this situation, we find we have reasons to fight the secular story that extend beyond merely championing a biblical ethic. We have a message that provides a much sturdier foundation for identity than that which can be accomplished by alternative means. Considering that some of the issues surrounding sexual identity and preferences these days can be perplexing, it is worth giving a brief treatment to the history that has led up to the contemporary ideas of sexual preferences, the LGBTQ+ movement, and the increasing attention given to transgenderism.

In his recent book, *The Rise and Triumph of the Modern Self*, Carl Trueman provides a well-crafted and extensively-researched treatment of the ways American culture has developed over the last two hundred years. He explores the philosophical, social, and political developments that have led to our current day when the sentence, "I am a man trapped in a woman's body," makes sense.

After clearly affirming the importance of the church teaching biblical sexuality, Trueman urges Christians to see this discussion taps into things much deeper than mere sexual ethics. "The LGBTQ+ discussion," he writes, "connects to matters of identity, of who we think we are at the most basic level. And the problem is that expressive individualism, manifested as sexual identity, is the way the world shapes us all."[6]

---

6. Carl Trueman, *The Rise and Triumph of the Modern Self* (Wheaton, IL: Crossway, 2020), 390.

I recommend that any reader interested in this topic make sure to read Trueman's book to get the full treatment of his argument. However, I want to focus in on this sexual-identity element of his work because it is immediately pertinent to seeing beyond the sexual ethics that are debated in the public square and in the church to the pressing gospel-level issues. This is important because some American evangelicals find themselves scratching their heads and wondering how we got to this point in history where gender refers to something more than the biological binary known throughout human history. In fact, I believe we as Christians have theological reasons to see that these "new" concepts are simply a new iteration of an essential human condition.

Idolatry and Autonomy

Being on the Bible faculty at Cedarville University, I have the privilege of teaching an undergraduate theology course that covers, among other things, the doctrine of humanity and the doctrine of sin. As we transition between these two doctrines, I spend some time lecturing through Genesis 3. Usually, I instruct the students to read Genesis 3:1–7, and I ask them to answer the question, "What was Eve reaching for?"

I want them to see that the fruit Eve plucked from the tree was merely a delivery vehicle for what she was really seeking: autonomy. The promise of the serpent was that if Adam and Eve ate the fruit, they would be like God. Though they were the only part of God's creation made in his image, they still faced the temptation of being *more* God-like. In other words, if they became gods, they would be able to call the shots for themselves instead of submitting to God's rule. This is autonomy—self-rule.

In breaking this commandment, Adam and Eve sought to become the rulers of their own lives. In so doing, they demonstrated they had deemed themselves to be most worthy of their ultimate allegiance. In a sense, they chose to worship themselves. The first idolatry.

Having seen that the allure exceeded the flavor of the fruit, I point out that every sin since that time has been another iteration of this same temptation to make ourselves god. Knowing what God has said, we persist in following our own wisdom. We seek autonomy from God's authority, and we bristle against anything that might impede upon our right to make much of ourselves. Nothing will be allowed to impinge upon our own freely determined pursuit of what we hope will satisfy us.

This manifests itself in a society that prizes individual sexual gratification over the designer's design for how it was intended to be pursued. It manifests itself in a culture that has sought to permit any variations of such pursuits that seem right in the eyes of the participants. Though the manifestations may seem increasingly strange to onlookers, they stem from the same fundamental desire to assert oneself as sovereign.

Peering Past Pleasure and Finding a Firm Foundation

Now, I want to pause for a moment here to recognize that sin has had a disordering effect on all of creation. This includes the order of the material world and our relationship to and perception of it. In such a sin-tainted environment, some people struggle with broken and disjointed relationships between the bodies they inhabit and to which they are attracted or their internal perceptions of themselves. A person struggling with such a condition is not—simply by experiencing this struggle—sinning as much as they are experiencing the disruption that sin has introduced into creation.[7]

The point of this section is not to infer that those who struggle with homosexual temptations or gender dysphoric confusions are somehow more sinful than those who struggle with extramarital heterosexual lust. Instead, I include this section to show the ways our culture is intent on fusing a person's identity with their pursuit of sexual satisfaction. This insistence is simply the sexualization of the search for autonomy and the worship of self.

The cultural current sweeps people away into thinking their sexual preferences or self-perceptions suffice as foundations upon which to build their identity. In addition to the harm that always comes from the disordered use of God's creation, we need to see the missionary encounter with this aspect of society taking us much deeper than the debate over sexual ethics.

In fact, out of compassion for our neighbors, we need to recognize that many wrestling with same-sex attraction or gender dysphoria report experiencing suffering, frustration, and alienation—both real and perceived—within society and

---

7. For more on this issue, see the helpful chapter "Same-Sex Attraction and Gender Dysphoria" in Robert Jones, Kristin Kellen, and Rob Green, *The Gospel for Disordered Lives: An Introduction to Christ-Centered Biblical Counseling* (Nashville: B&H Academic, 2021), 399–408.

churches.[8] Biblical counselor and author Kristin Kellen writes of her experience counseling individuals going through this type of suffering:

> As I (Kristin) have sat repeatedly with counselees who struggle in these areas, I've been astounded by the depth of their suffering. It may be because of rejection from loved ones, including those in the church, a constant feeling of disconnect with their own bodies, or hopelessness. While (same-sex attraction) and (gender dysphoria) are their "presenting problems," their pervasive feelings involve suffering, which the Bible addresses at great length.[9]

If, then, the church intends to have a missiological engagement with the culture within the context of discussions of sexual identity, we must be quick to meet and comfort people when their

---

8. Of course, not everyone who experiences same-sex attraction or gender dysphoria will report frustration or negative emotions associated with their sexual or gender identity. However, there appears to be data to demonstrate the prevalence among LGBTQ populations of such feelings of social isolation. See, for example, the survey of data produced by Jonathan Garcia, Nancy Vargas, Jesse L. Clark, Mario Magaña Álvarez, Devynne A. Nelons, and Richard G. Parker, "Social Isolation and Connectedness as Determinants of Well-Being: Global Evidence Mapping Focused on LGBTQ Youth," *Glob Public Health* 15, no. 4 (2020): 497–519, which demonstrates the propensity for LGBTQ youth to report experiencing social isolation in connection with their sexual preferences or transgender identities.

9. Jones, Kellen, and Green, *The Gospel for Disordered Lives*, 402.

sexuality fails to provide a strong enough foundation to support their identities.

The church must provide a compelling vision of a more trustworthy foundation for understanding ourselves. We must be able to demonstrate the sturdiness of a God-given identity in contrast to a do-it-yourself identity. Thus, we need to do more than just proclaim where sexual idolatry leads away from God's law. We need to address the futility of trying to make ourselves according to our own image. We must show there is beauty in embracing our createdness because our dignity, worth, and purpose are given qualities bestowed upon us by our Creator.[10]

As those who have a missionary longing for people to flourish by embracing the gospel, we need to be able to paint a more biblical and compelling picture of where human identity comes from. This can address the root idolatry that produces the unsatisfying fruit of the world's ever-broadening sexual ethic. As Kellen encourages us, we need to speak to the beauty of the fact that "The believer's identity is

> **We need to do more than just proclaim where sexual idolatry leads away from God's law. We need to address the futility of trying to make ourselves according to our own image.**

---

10. To this point of the givenness of our identities, I would highly recommend readers work through the excellent volume by Kelly Kapic, *You're Only Human: How Your Limits Reflect God's Design and How That's Good News* (Grand Rapids: Brazos, 2022).

found in Christ. He, rather than our feelings or struggles, determines what we are."[11]

But if we are to begin this task of addressing the idol of self-making through sexual exploration, we must begin with cutting off the idolatrous roots we bring into the sanctuary.

Sex Talk: Idols in the Sanctuary

I've already said that the sexual idolatry flaunted by secular society is not merely an outside-the-church reality. The same siren song sung by secular culture is sometimes hummed by Christians while we construct ethical barriers around the outside of the shrine.

I want to be absolutely clear I am not criticizing biblical sexual standards. Sex is a part of God's world to be enjoyed within the context of covenanted marriage between one man and one woman. A biblical sexual ethic is part of God's world that he declared to be very good.

However, while sex within these biblical parameters is good, it is not god.

As you read the previous sentence you might dismiss it as obvious. Yet, I am afraid that we in the church have sometimes labored to construct a biblical fence around a cultural understanding of sex as ultimate. Against strong cultural pressures to abandon the "antiquated" and "puritanical" ideas about sexual norms, we affirm biblical teaching about sex and marriage. But too often

---

11. Jones, Kellen, and Green, *The Gospel for Disordered Lives*, 403.

we silently still believe married sex will provide the same ultimate satisfaction that the culture promises through more promiscuous means.

The wreckage of our failure to confront an idolatrous vision of sex can be seen when young Christians who were virgins at the altar are divorced before their first anniversary. They may have kept biblical standards prior to making their marriage vows, but they brought the baggage of the world's expectations for sexual fulfillment into their marriage bed.

The Bible presents an identity for humans that far outstrips any form of a shallow and shoddy identity that could be cobbled together by one's sexual appetite, conquests, and preferences. This is true and it is beautiful when compared to the buyer's remorse experienced following a one-night stand or a shame-filled reflection on a relationship that went too far. But we must not miss the fact that, for us to actually hold out a more compelling and sturdy identity to people, we must first believe it for ourselves. And that means we need to be speaking and teaching about sex in ways that clearly appreciate it for what it is while not presenting it as something it is not.

One way we do this is by taking seriously some of the concerns that have been raised about so-called "purity culture." The phrase "purity culture" has been used as a negative label for some ways of teaching teenagers about the importance of sexual purity that inadvertently present protecting one's virginity as the highest aim of an unmarried teen. Often the promise of a better sex life within the bounds of marriage is held up as the reward for those who reach the altar in a state of sexual purity. Purity rings, chastity vows, and sundry shame-inducing images of those who forfeit their virgin-status prior to marriage have been critiqued for how they affect young people's views of sex. One person's reflection on the phenomenon is that purity culture is "the well-meaning desire for protection with a list of what-to-do's buried among deficient whys."[12]

"Purity culture" has also garnered attention due to the public deconstruction stories told by its former champions. In some circles, this discussion has become unwieldy and unhelpful as people throw out the baby of biblical teaching with the bathwater of poor expression.[13] But there remain very helpful voices that both affirm a biblical sexual ethic and call for a more chastened approach to our rhetoric regarding chastity.

One of the most helpful of these voices, Rachel Welcher, wrote a book entitled, *Talking Back to Purity Culture*. Motivated by "righteous anger at a Christian subculture that, for years, has made false promises and worshiped the idol of chastity rather than the Lord Jesus Christ," Welcher—rather than merely focusing on sexual purity—calls readers to pursue biblical sexuality as a subset of the larger pursuit of holiness.[14]

---

12. As cited from Brianna Lambert's Twitter response to Rachel Welcher in Welcher's book, *Talking Back to Purity Culture: Rediscovering Faithful Christian Sexuality* (Downers Grove, IL: IVP, 2020), 14.

13. For instance, Nadia Bolz-Weber prescribes a biblically unjustifiable sexual permissiveness as the antidote for what she sees as the shameful symptoms of purity culture in her recent book, *Shameless: A Sexual Reformation* (New York: Convergent Books, 2019). Bolz-Weber is an example of a biblically dismissive reactionary whose proposals wander well beyond the bounds of biblical teaching.

14. Welcher, *Talking Back to Purity Culture*, 9.

Welcher responds to those who have rejected both purity culture and biblical boundaries for sexuality with a tender rebuke, writing, "Beloved, do not be deceived by such thinking. The gospel of self is everywhere, and it tastes sweet, like wine. Which is why we must drink all the more deeply of God's Word."[15] She goes on to specify what the Word tells us about our purpose and how it both includes and transcends our sexual ethics, writing, "When we start calling holy what God calls sinful, we have ceased to honor him. We have misunderstood what holiness means. Holiness is not premarital sex without shame. Holiness is God, the Lord Almighty, who was, and is, and is to come."[16]

Throughout the book, Welcher remains firm in her convictions: extra-marital sexual activity is sin, including pornography use, lust, and all forms of physical sexual acts. Yet she is also clear that forgiveness of sexual sin is available in Christ. Her concern is that occasionally our messaging ends up omitting the fact that purification for all of our sexual sin is only available through repentance and under Christ's blood. Still, she is also very clear that our messaging should never lead us to believe our purity is available by simply making it to the altar as virgins.

Welcher reorients the discussion of sex by connecting it to the more holistic call to holiness, our inability to meet that standard, and Christ's righteousness and purity extended to us in the gospel. She writes,

---

15. Welcher, *Talking Back to Purity Culture*, 134.
16. Welcher, *Talking Back to Purity Culture*, 135.

God's sexual ethic is first meant to reveal our sin as "utterly sinful" (Romans 7:13) and to devastate us into acknowledging our need for a Savior. . . . The main point is not pursuing sexual purity but recognizing our desperate need for Christ. So many of us walked right past the gospel on our way to a purity conference. . . . We wore purity rings as badges of honor, forgetting that it is Jesus who cleanses us from all unrighteousness.[17]

She concludes this section with what I think is the most pressing aspect of the discussion: "The Christian pursuit of sexual purity is biblical, but it *must* flow out of a recognition that it is Jesus who makes us pure."[18]

I would love to go back to my early years and speak this gospel-centered message to myself as a teen. I vividly remember praying that Jesus would not return until after I was married. I was so bought into the promise that fulfillment would come through the consummation of my marriage that I wanted the maker of my soul to hold off on the consummation of the ages. Something is desperately wrong with that way of thinking.

While this reflection may evoke a chuckle and maybe even a memory that many readers can relate to, it is actually a sobering glimpse into the idolatry to which I had given myself over. I mean, think about it. I had so imbibed the idea that sex was the pinnacle of human existence that I prayed for the delay of

---

17. Welcher, *Talking Back to Purity Culture*, 137.
18. Welcher, *Talking Back to Purity Culture*, 137.

the new creation. In my heart I had preferred the allure of sexual satisfaction to what should be the goal of my soul: immediate and unmediated communion with the triune God.

Come to think of it, how many times from the pulpit or in ministry settings have you heard the same sentiment? Maybe it comes in the form of jokes that are told about hoping someone gets married before Jesus comes back, or perhaps it's an off-handed reference to praying there will be sex in heaven. These ideas usually come from a place of well-meaning levity. However, they simply reinforce that our hopes and expectations for fulfillment have not freed themselves from the promise of sex to deliver satisfaction. Taking a glimpse at our American evangelical bedroom through the idol-identifying lenses of a missionary, it seems that we have work to do.

A Satisfying Kingdom and the Idol-Smashing King

From a missionary perspective, wherever we find worship being directed toward that which is not God, we have gospel work to do. As we consider the way we address the issues of sexual identity in the broader world, we must do so with the sober recognition that sex and sexual fulfillment are flimsy foundations incapable of sustaining the weight of identity.

In all the ways we may be tempted to address the unbiblical and unbridled sexual revelry of our lost neighbors and friends, we do

> **Sex and sexual fulfillment are flimsy foundations incapable of sustaining the weight of identity.**

well to pause and consider the suffering that comes from such a frustrating pursuit. Instead of beginning with the sinful nature of extra-biblical sexual exploration, it may be most loving to help our lost friends see the futility of their attempts to construct an identity around something so fleeting as sexual pleasure.

A More Satisfying Story: Compassionate Evangelism

This compassionate evangelism can be accomplished in loving conversations and relationships where you can take the opportunity to ask probing questions. You might get at the heart of the matter by asking something like the following questions:

- Do you think that people were meant to be defined by their sexual appetites?
- Doesn't sex seem like too small of a thing to build someone's identity on?
- Don't you think we are worth more than whatever pleasure we can get?
- Do you find it exhausting to make and define yourself from the ground up?

Asked in the context of genuine compassion for those who may be deeply hurting or exhausted, these questions can open the door to opportunities for presenting the beauty of the given identity provided in Scripture.

After all, with our missionary lenses on, we are reminded that legislating biblical sexuality does not draw people closer to Jesus. And even if we convince someone of the goodness of our biblically informed sexual ethic, we have not addressed the core problems that arise from idolatry in the human heart.

Before we give someone biblical ethics, we must give them biblical hope. Before we instruct someone about the role of sex in God's good creation, we must introduce them to the goodness of God displayed in Christ. Before we hold someone to gospel-living, we must hold out the eternal life of the gospel itself.

If Christian living is only possible as a Holy Spirit-empowered response to the grace of God in Christ, then we must be wary of holding our gospel-less friends and neighbors to Christian standards of living prior to introducing them to Christ.

This is not a call to compromise on biblical sexuality. Nor is it a call to acquiesce to laws and legislations that expose vulnerable members of society to unnecessary danger—physically or emotionally. Christians should be actively engaged in supporting measures to protect children—whether in bathrooms or classrooms—from predatory behavior exposing them to sexual activity or sexual ideology that exceeds their maturity.

However, this chapter is a reminder that in our interpersonal relationships with non-Christians who are struggling with sexual identity or sexual revelry, we need to engage at a level deeper than mere sexual ethics. We must address the idolatrous tendencies that misdirect our worship. Our primary need—whether homosexual, heterosexual, or attempting to create a new category of sexual identity—is to have restored hearts that are purified by Jesus, instructed by the Holy Spirit and the illumination of the Word, and redirected toward the God of the universe.

Idol-Smashing through a Worship-Driven Sexual Ethic

As we have noted throughout this chapter, missionaries are trained to do a sort of theological triage among people who are inevitably caught up in various idolatries. Each culture will present an array of its own expression of sinful behaviors, but missionary training involves tracing the behavior back to a root idolatry. Rather than merely offering a corrective to actions and behaviors that fall outside of the biblical standard, missionaries attempt to find ways to present the gospel as a more fulfilling, satisfying alternative to the story told by cultural idols. While this idolatry-identification may be easier to do outside of the church as we find more and more examples of sexualized self-making, we must address the ways we have first moralized our own dalliances with sexual idolatry.

Our missionary lenses help us to be attentive to where our fleshly sexual idolatry has been smuggled in behind our biblically protected sexual prudence. But what steps can we take to smash the idol of sexual fulfillment rather than just domesticating it behind biblical boundaries? I think contemporary authors such as Rachel Welcher have begun offering some very helpful corrective proposals for how the church speaks about sex that get to the root of our idolatry while still upholding the biblical teaching about sex.

I believe the church—from youth group discussions all the way to the pulpit—would do well to intentionally put sex in its place. This includes teaching a biblical sexual ethic, but goes beyond it to helping people in the church assess their own hearts as to what place sex is given in their lives and thoughts. We might ask people to reflect on the following questions:

- Would you trust God if he called you to a life of singleness?
- Do you believe that satisfaction with your life requires sexual fulfillment?
- As you prepare for marriage, how much does sex consume your planning?
- How much does your sex life affect your affection for your spouse?

These questions and others like them aim to push beyond just the discipline required of Christians to keep biblical boundaries before marriage and to tap into the deeper heart motivations. They aim to show that we could remain physically chaste while committing spiritual adultery by worshipping the promise of sex in place of God.

Not only will these sorts of questions help expose idolatry in our midst, but they might also help shape the way we teach and preach about sex—again, from youth group to pulpit. Before teaching on the topic of sex, a pastor or ministry leader might ask themselves some clarifying questions:

- Does this application challenge or reinforce the cultural promise of fulfillment through sexual satisfaction?
- Does this sermon encourage single members to see themselves as whole amidst celibacy?

- Have I communicated that sexual idolatry needs to be rooted out of both singleness and marriage?
- Have I presented sexual ethics as a worship issue or as mere moralism?

These types of reflective questions can help pastors and youth leaders communicate the proper place of sex and also the proper expectations of what sex can and cannot provide. This is an important message for those of us prone to idol-making, and those of us who live in a world increasingly intent on making pleasure the pinnacle of human purpose—that is to say, *all* of us.

In the end, as we look at our world and our church through missionary lenses, our concern to uphold a biblical sexual ethic should be shaped by the gospel that we both hold out and attempt to live out. This involves speaking to our unbelieving friends with the compassion that recognizes the futility of trying to define themselves by our own pleasures and personalities. It also includes working with one another as believers as we continue the heart-level work of crushing the idol of sex in our midst. Our message within the church should be one that reminds us nothing short of God is worthy of worship. Seeing sex as a potential source of idolatry is the first step toward recognizing ways we remain prone to directing our worship toward lesser things.

Our missionary task involves allowing the gospel to challenge all worldly kings and kingdoms. No idol can provide the good life that it promises, nor can it be baptized with religious rules. In the end, no idols can stand before King Jesus—whether they are idols in the world or idols in the sanctuary. Just like my parents' house, American evangelicals need to make sure the bed we display doesn't overwhelm its place in the bedroom.

Chapter 6

Our Yard

Manicured vs. Missional

After having worked our way through the inside of the house, we made our way outside to survey the backyard. The over-extended springs on the screen door gave their familiar metallic screech as I walked out into the now-empty territory that had played host to summer birthday parties, innumerable games of hide-and-seek, and hours spent enjoying every ounce of fun that could be wrung out of our budget version of an above-ground pool.

But the memories that stuck out most were the countless games of backyard basketball played against my dad in that space. I looked up to see if the floodlights we had installed still adorned the back porch. Those lights were added to facilitate our night games, much to the dismay of the neighbors. Long after sunset, our neighbors were forced to put up with the sound of uneven dribbling, shots clanging off the rim, and my exasperated cries of disbelief when Dad's trusty fade-away shot brought an end to yet another intense battle.

Eventually I got to the point where my skills and height overtook my dad and the games were a bit more evenly matched. But regardless of who won, I knew even at the time that something deeper was going on. I was being invested in. I was being formed as a man. I was being discipled by my dad on that hand-poured concrete slab.

I stood there remembering the day that we turned our backyard into this basketball court. I was fairly young, but my parents wanted to encourage my growing interest in basketball. Even though my mom really enjoyed keeping up the flower beds around the backyard and my dad was regimented in keeping the lawn looking nice, they decided to dig up almost all the grass in order to pour the slab and put up a basketball goal for me.

Watching my parents make that first selfless choice of sacrificing the yard for their kids began a process of forming me. But the process continued every time Dad got home from work, threw down his briefcase, and immediately called for the ball I was bouncing while squaring up for a jump shot.

I knew my dad had just spent ten hours working. But I also could see in his eyes that spending time with me was a conscious choice he wanted to make even at the end of a long day. In between games while we caught our breath, he would take time to talk to me about life and faith, winning and losing, grit and determination. On one hand, we were just playing basketball. But on the other hand, I knew I was being invested in by the man who took seriously his responsibility to raise me, train me, shape me, and launch me into the world.

I grabbed a ball sitting off to the side of the court and took a shot that was as rusty as the pole holding up the hoop. As the ball clanged off the backboard, it rolled off into a patch of weeds alongside the garage. Reaching down to grab the ball, I chuckled as I saw half-buried in the dirt a yellowed plastic tag from one of the perennials my mom had tried to plant there one spring. Those flowers were always fated to meet an early demise as errant shots crushed them into the ground, but still I can't remember a time my mom fussed at me for it. She—like my dad—was more concerned to invest in our use of the space than in its appearance.

The realtor's photographer was going to have to work to make this yard look attractive to a potential buyer. By digging up the grass and pouring the cement, my parents had sacrificed their opportunity to make our lot attractive to onlookers and passersby. Though the yard suffered aesthetically, they saw this space as something to be stewarded as an investment in their kids. Standing there and reflecting on all that this place represented to me, I couldn't imagine it being any more beautiful even if it was overflowing with blossoming flower beds and a lush lawn.

Marketing Methods or Biblical Ministry

My parents were convinced that the mission of our backyard was to be a place where life happened. They knew if we were to enjoy this space, it would be more messy than manicured. The purpose of this place was to be where the family played, partied, and prayed together. Thus, their grass might not have the opportunity to grow full and healthy, but their children would.

As we inspect the American church and its understanding of ministry, it is worth asking: Do we invest more in manicure or mission?

I fear that many American churches have been wooed by the short-term explosive growth promised by flashy and fresh marketing methods rather than being convinced of the long-term impact of sustained, "ordinary" patterns of local, biblical ministry and disciple-making. We've been told that growth and impact come after we develop the right branding, logos, and platforms. And of course, we need to fill that platform with someone who will serve as an icon to carry the brand—a charismatic leader whose celebrity can earn a broad hearing and whose image can represent our impact.

While I am concerned that this marketing-driven philosophy of ministry often results in diminishing life-on-life discipleship in a church, I also believe this image-making contributes to some of the most heartbreaking and gospel-shaming instances of ministry failure.

One of the greatest disappointments and heartaches that the church of Jesus Christ can experience is a pastor disqualifying himself from ministry. In recent years an overwhelming number of such stories have made headlines. Some of these disqualifications were rooted in all-too-common sexual sin, while others were due to financial mismanagement and greed. Still others have disqualified themselves by prideful, self-important, domineering approaches to leadership. Repeatedly reading the news about leadership failures within American churches over the last few years has been absolutely heartbreaking.

Now, to be sure, some tabloids and blogs have at times cast undue aspersions on ministers for the sake of a titillating story and click-bait. We do well in any such discussions to heed the important instruction of 1 Timothy 5:19: "Don't accept an accusation against an elder unless it is supported by two or three witnesses." Any such false reports aside, however, there have been far too many cases in which the substantiated failings of leaders in the American church have brought shame to the gospel.

> **One of the greatest disappointments and heartaches that the church of Jesus Christ can experience is a pastor disqualifying himself from ministry.**

As these stories of well-known figures in American evangelicalism have emerged, I have heard several fellow church members asking the question, "What is causing this? How did we get here?" While there are any number of answers that each individual case might provide, I fear some of the cause can be traced back to consumer Christians. We have perpetuated the idea that ministry can take its cues from marketing. If we create a celebrity spokesperson and a platform for them, the gospel will spread more rapidly. In pursuit of this vision, we have grown adept at creating celebrities. But all too often celebrity hampers the "taking on the form of a servant" required of Philippians 2 ministers. In many cases, chasing and maintaining celebrity precedes disqualification.

As has been the case throughout this book, I believe Lesslie Newbigin's missionary lenses and his example will help us glimpse some of the ways that common, American ideas of ministry and ministers have contributed to such ministry failures.

Newbigin's Missionary Church and Example

While influenced by his experience in the churches of his youth, Newbigin's approach to gospel ministry was formed and forged during his forty years as a missionary. Throughout his time in India, Newbigin became familiar with various approaches to the practical work of evangelism, discipleship, and church planting. His work with the World Council of Churches further exposed him to diverse philosophies of ministry and missionary methods that were practiced globally. He encountered advocates of the Church Growth Movement whose methods promised rapid growth. He spoke with people who sought to encourage common ground and interfaith dialogue. And he felt the draw of defaulting to traditional ministry patterns in and among new churches in new contexts.

Still, despite access to numerous ministry methods, Newbigin remained singularly focused on drawing his philosophy from the Bible's holistic view of the church and its missionary vocation.[1] Newbigin resisted the allure of methods that compromised the

---

1. The language of missionary vocation of the church owes itself to the helpful summary of Newbigin's contributions written by Michael Goheen, *The Church and Its Vocation: Lesslie Newbigin's Missionary Ecclesiology* (Grand Rapids: Baker, 2018).

gospel to gain a broader hearing. He refused to embrace strategies that drew more from multi-level marketing programs than from biblical patterns.

Convinced that the church was God's "Plan A" for his kingdom's advance, Newbigin saw at least three "ordinary" ways the Bible determines how a church is to operate as a corporate body of individual Christians who "take enduring responsibility for a particular area."[2] First, *the church is to be the humble servant of Jesus for its neighbors by taking on the tasks and posture of a gospel servant.* Newbigin saw this working out in the combination of mercy ministry and verbal gospel proclamation: "Verbal witness to Christ and his Cross is needed if people's deepest needs are to be met. Conversion to God's saving reign is most credibly invited when the followers of Jesus follow their Master's example in stooping down and washing feet."[3]

> **A gospel that requires self-sacrifice does not get airtime in a world of self-comfort.**

Washing feet is not flashy. Repentance is not marketable. And a gospel that requires self-sacrifice does not get airtime in a world of self-comfort. But it is the example and invitation of our Lord, and therefore, servanthood should mark our ministry.

---

2. This statement and the following three notions of ministry method are adapted slightly from the summary statement of Newbigin's philosophy as recorded by his biographer, Geoffrey Wainwright, in *Lesslie Newbigin: A Theological Life* (Eugene, OR: Wipf & Stock, 2000), 144.

3. Wainwright, *Lesslie Newbigin: A Theological Life*, 145.

Second, *the church must point beyond itself as a witness to Jesus and his kingdom*. This means the church and its ministries should not exist to prop itself up or its own glory. Rather, all church ministries should point to the kingdom of God and his sovereign reign on display in their midst. The church should never so prioritize its own perpetuation that it prefers worldly marketing tactics to its biblically prescribed purpose of pointing to King Jesus and his kingdom.

And third, *the church is to have an intercessory and priestly relationship to its neighbors*. This requires bringing both compassion and confrontation into the neighborhood. It will express itself in love to neighbors who are far from God while never compromising the truth of the gospel that challenges all rival kingdoms. This vision of the church's purpose helps to remove the temptation to see the church as either a private social club or as a group whose primary goal is merely to attract as many as possible.

These three biblical notions in themselves challenge some of our approaches to the church and its collective mission. But even beyond his teaching, Newbigin also exemplified these principles in his personal ministry. Whether a church member or a church leader, I believe the following three insights from Newbigin's missionary example can help us fight against the contemporary allure of celebrity and platform as pathways to success in ministry.

A Persistent Focus on People

Just as Newbigin taught that the local church is for a particular place and its people, so too was his ministry marked by a personal focus on the particular people to whom he was ministering. That there were people who had not yet heard the name of the God in whose image they were made was a reality that burdened Newbigin. It was his heart for people that sent him to the mission field in the first place.

But beyond his initial missionary motivation, "people" did not remain a vague idea for Newbigin. Nor could "people" be boiled down to faceless numbers of those impacted by his ministry. People, for Newbigin, were individual image-bearers—future brothers and sisters in Christ and those who bore God's image but had yet to repent and believe—who Newbigin saw, invested in, and sought to care for. We can see how Newbigin genuinely valued individual people as we read how he described being appalled at the interaction between missionaries and Indians, writing,

> I couldn't help being horrified by the sort of relation that seems to exist between the missionaries and the people. It seems so utterly remote from the New Testament. . . . We drove up like lords in a car, soaking everybody else with mud on the way, and then carry on a sort of inspection, finding all the faults we can, putting everyone through their paces. They all sort of stand at attention and say, "Sir." It's *awful*.[4]

---

4. As quoted in Paul Weston, ed., *Lesslie Newbigin: Missionary Theologian* (Grand Rapids: Eerdmans, 2006), 6.

Newbigin does not here comment on how his ministry approach was affected by this experience apart from noting that he was appalled. However, it is clear that his vision of the people of India—and people in general—was different than that of his colleagues. He was averse to any suggestion or indication that he, as a foreign missionary, existed on a higher plane or was worthy of greater respect than his Indian brothers and sisters. As Newbigin urged the church to take the posture of foot-washing servants, he also demonstrated a life convinced that one cannot minister as a servant and maintain a distance from people's feet.

Missions—like all gospel ministry—is inextricably tied to working with people and helping them see and live the beauty of the gospel in the messiness of their everyday lives. If that is the case, then any methodology or ministry plan that causes ministers to withdraw or remain remote from those they are serving requires significant inspection. We will return to investigate where current ministry models encourage remote ministry later in this chapter, but before that, Newbigin provides us a second example of self-forgetfulness in the service not just of people, but of Christ's kingdom.

A Consistent Consciousness of Conversion

The second ministry example Newbigin provides for us is that he never allowed his international ministry and renown to eclipse his singular focus on serving the kingdom of God. While invitations to speak at important global gatherings might have presented temptations to Newbigin to build his own kingdom, his humble awareness of the miracle of his own conversion kept him from seeking to increase his own reputation, notoriety, and fame.

This facet of Newbigin's example struck me as I was reading through his biography. Following a quote where Newbigin connected his conversion with his commission, his biographer Geoffrey Wainwright writes the following stunning summary of Newbigin's deepest ministry motivations:

> Lesslie Newbigin benefitted from a lasting conversion; he interpreted that blessing as for the sake of others. His life in the Spirit from whom he received many gifts found outward expression in powerful testimony and in compassionate service. This was a holy man whose plain and humble character attracted many—not, ultimately, to him, but rather through him—to the Source of his and all holiness.[5]

I cannot think of a more desirable way to describe the life of a Christian who was entrusted influence in ministry than to say that he ministered out of a consciousness of his own conversion. Such a disposition stands sadly in contrast with some of the examples of ministers who have proven to be more prima donna than pastor in recent years.

Instead of being driven by strategies to increase his influence, Newbigin's ministry was conditioned by being ever aware that he

---

5. Wainwright, *Lesslie Newbigin: A Theological Life*, 392.

was undeserving of the salvation he enjoyed. His appreciation of his own conversion naturally flowed into his ministry as a commission to invest in and invite others into Christ's kingdom. Whatever level of fame or influence he might achieve, Newbigin was aware that no kingdom he could construct for himself would hold a candle to the kingdom of God and its advance through the church.

This leads to the third way we can learn from Newbigin's missionary example. While Newbigin was invested in global projects and partnerships, he was unshakably convinced that the kingdom of God is advancing through the vehicle of local churches.

A Commitment to the Church

If you were to flip through the pages of Newbigin's biography and his writings, you would find that some discussion of the church features on nearly every page. While evangelism, cultural assessment, and ecumenism were prevalent themes and interests throughout Newbigin's life, they were only of interest insofar as they emerged from his reflections on and commitment to the biblical teaching about the church. He was thoroughly convinced that the mission of God, whose climax had come in Christ, will continue properly through Christ's church.

This perspective remained consistent in Newbigin's ministry even after he had left the work of church planting and strengthening in India for England. Having retired from the mission field and taken a prestigious teaching post, Newbigin resigned the post after only a few years to take on a pastoral role in a dying parish church on the verge of having to close its doors. True to his under-standing of the church as a humble servant of the people in its neighborhood, Newbigin's personal ministry example remained doggedly committed to the local church and its ministry to indi-vidual people.

These three biblical principles guided Newbigin's reflection on the church in theory, but they also shaped his ministry in prac-tice. While it may seem rather simple—perhaps even simplistic—to offer these three guiding thoughts as missionary insights for ministry, they stand in sharp contrast to some of the tendencies in American ministry methods today.

Now, to demonstrate the value of Newbigin's insights, it would be easy to pick apart some of the more famous examples of mega-ministries that have imploded due to celebrity pastor fail-ures. But I think it might be more helpful to reflect a little closer to where many in ministry find themselves. Most readers do not have thousands of people attending their church and download-ing their podcasts, so it might be easier to write off the pursuit of celebrity as a problem for those who already have it. Instead, I want to investigate some more common ways these temptations toward kingdom building presented themselves to me upon my return to the United States.

Coming Home to New Temptations

When my wife and I lived in the Middle East, we lived in total obscurity. Well, in one sense, that's not actually true. I am a six-foot-three white man who was living in a land where the average height of the olive-skinned population is around five and a half feet. So, I was actually very conspicuous within our community. What I mean by "total obscurity" is not that we were unknown, but that we were uninfluential.

On the field we spent hours daily sharing the beauty of the gospel with those who we longed to see grasp it. And though they were glad to talk about our faith with us, time after time our pleas were disregarded. It would have taken an absurd level of self-deception for us to view ourselves as community influencers. Any fame I might have enjoyed was only due to the superficial novelty of being a relative giant who could speak Arabic. The thing I would have most wanted to be famous for—the ability to give a convincing and articulate defense of the gospel—was actually what my friends and neighbors dismissed about me.

In addition to usually being far removed from celebrity, those who are compelled to go to the mission field are rarely the types of people who are prone to seeking status and the esteem of leadership titles. Those who were given leadership roles laughed at the idea that there was any prestige involved in their role, saying, "Promotion means more work, more responsibility, more headache, and exactly the same pay." During our time on the field, then, we faced no temptation to try to impress the right people nor was there any incentive or desire to chase promotion.

Furthermore, because the public nature of social media posed a threat to our gospel work in a country where it was illegal, my social media influence extended only as far as my family members who visited my Facebook page to see pictures of our kids. In fact, the only reason I signed up for a Twitter account was for security reasons. Twitter served as a useful tool for getting minute-by-minute updates on where the most violent protests were occurring in our city so I could avoid them while running errands. I lived in obscurity of influence in our country and online.

For all those reasons, when we transitioned back to the United States and I began to teach, I was unprepared for the degree to which my heart responded sinfully to the approval my students gave me simply by writing down the things that I said. When invitations to preach, or to speak on a podcast, or write for various publications arrived in my in-box, I found myself entertaining new thoughts of self-importance. And my wandering heart began to imagine the potential of gaining a voice and establishing myself as an expert with influence.

The obscurity that I had lived in on the field was no longer possible by virtue of my position at a university. I was caught off guard by the litany of temptations that came with even the smallest of recognitions of my work. I began discovering in myself some of the ugly sinful tendencies toward self-importance that had laid dormant or been beaten down over the years of facing regular reminders that I was anything but an influencer.

And while I quickly identified the sinful way my thoughts wandered selfward, I admit to beginning to think maybe building my kingdom and reputation was not at odds with building God's kingdom. The thought crossed my mind, "The bigger the platform I can build—by networking with the right people, garnering a following on social media, and securing public recognition—the broader my influence for the kingdom can be." I was inclined to think that perhaps the best way to serve the Lord was to serve my own brand. If I invest in my own platform, then I can better plat-form the Lord. If I build my own kingdom, then it will provide greater opportunity to build God's kingdom.

The logic of these arguments seems sturdy enough. If I can draw more attention to myself, it follows that I can draw more attention to my message. If I garner more of an audience, I have the ability to garner a greater hearing for the gospel. But the sneaky thing of it is this logic builds on a worldly vision for mar-keting rather than building on the biblical vision of making dis-ciples by washing feet, teaching the Word, and clinging to Jesus.[6]

And the biblical method for making disciples looks much more like what we saw from Newbigin than what we see in mass marketing.[7] Jesus did not commis-sion us to go and make platforms, making much of our name prior to making much of his name. He charged his church with making disciples indiscriminately of all people by baptizing them into the

> **I was inclined to think that perhaps the best way to serve the Lord was to serve my own brand.**

---

6. A beautiful example of this simple, faithful vision of ministry can be found in the sage wisdom recorded by Harold Senkbeil, *The Care of Souls: Cultivating a Pastor's Heart* (Bellingham, WA: Lexham, 2019).

7. By the Lord's kindness, I picked up a book during my first semester that helped to identify the distinction between the way the world seeks to gain and use power for self-interest and how the kingdom of God employs power as modeled by Christ. While I read the first edition, I highly recommend reading the second edition of Jamin Goggin and Kyle Strobel, *The Way of the Dragon or the Way of the Lamb: Searching for Jesus' Path of Power in a Church That Has Abandoned It,* rev. and exp. (Nashville: Nelson, 2021).

triune Name and teaching total obedience to everything he commanded. The ministry entrusted to us by Christ in the Scriptures requires me to devote myself much more to what Newbigin exemplified than to seeking the attention of an influencer.

Inspecting Our American Yard

You might wonder why I, as a relatively unknown teacher at a small school in the cornfields of Ohio, spent time in this chapter divulging my own personal wrestling with temptations toward power and fame. One could argue it would have been better to chronicle the history and missteps leading to the fall of a well-known minister in order to warn others by way of a familiar story.[8] Such an approach would surely make its own contribution.

But the reason I chose to expose my own inner struggle is that I think it is far more common for a pastor of a middle-sized church to battle thoughts like mine than it is to relate to the struggles of men and women whose ministries already generate millions of dollars a year and whose names feature on every conference advertisement. My temptations came despite a lack of fame or name recognition. That means these temptations to kingdom-building can prove common and equally dangerous to those of us whose ministries will never reach national platforms.

---

8. I am not discounting the important warnings provided by the recent work of Mike Cosper and *Christianity Today* in the podcast, *The Rise and Fall of Mars Hill*. I found it to be a sobering warning to those who are trying to faithfully navigate the minefield that is contemporary ministry in America.

While few have to wrestle with the reality of celebrity in ministry, many experience its allure in ways that I described in my small corner of the ministry world. Since many will struggle with these temptations, I think it is helpful to revisit Newbigin's example and consider how it challenges certain aspects of contemporary American ministry. The first challenge Newbigin issues strikes at the tendency of Americans to value efficiency at the expense of relationship.

Maintaining a Persistent People-Focus

One of the things ingrained in me on the mission field was the importance of being present with the person in front of me. When I was sitting down to tea with a lost neighbor, he had my full attention because I knew he was throttling toward a Christless eternity. And given the lack of many other Christians in his country, if he didn't hear the gospel from me, there might not be another opportunity. If I let myself be distracted by the idea of the lost masses in other places, I would not be present enough to minister to this person across the table from me.

Even though our strategies were attentive to the millions of lost people around us, our daily ministry had to occur with individuals. We could develop great strategic plans for theoretically multiplying disciples, but if we weren't investing in actual relationships with individuals, there would be no disciples to multiply. No matter how good my ministry plan might have been, this person sitting across from me had to have my whole attention because people are the ministry.

When I turn to inspect our American church with these missionary lenses, several things stand out. First of all, the American church has invested a lot of time and effort in developing ministry structures that excel in efficiency. If someone wants to become a member of our church, we send them to a detailed page on our website where they can apply, watch some explanatory videos, and read our doctrinal statement. If someone is struggling with their marriage, we enroll them in a 13-week study on biblical marriage. If someone can't make it to physically join us during our Sunday gathering, we live-stream our services and avoid having to make visits to each shut-in to make them feel like they are still part of the church. Our ministries maximize efficiency in that they are easily reproducible, reach a wide audience, and maintain consistency.

> **We could develop great strategic plans for theoretically multiplying disciples, but if we weren't investing in actual relationships with individuals, there would be no disciples to multiply.**

The problem is that efficiency is often the enemy of relationship.

Relationships are rarely efficient because people are not discipled on an assembly line. Strategy and structure are necessary to facilitate ministry. But without direct investment in people a pastor becomes a strategist, not a minister. Likewise, strategy and structure provide efficient ways to pass people through programs and can help grow the size of the crowd, but if crowd growth results in a pastor being further and further removed from knowing the individuals who make up the crowd, there is a disconnect between efficiency and ministry.

Think back to the story of my yard. My parents wanted our backyard to be a place that facilitated and deepened our family relationship. To do so they sacrificed the appearance of the yard and invested in the structures necessary to turn it into a basketball court. Though our backyard court saved us from walking down to the school yard to play basketball every day, it was not merely designed for efficiency. The structure of the backyard basketball court was designed to amplify interpersonal relationship between us as we used it. We might ask whether our ministry structures are likewise designed to maximize relationship or efficiency.

Here are some diagnostic questions that might help apply some of this missionary insight to our American churches. As you read these questions, please don't take them to imply that all ministry structures or programs are at odds with relationship and meaningful ministry. Structures and programs can serve as funnels into relationship—especially for those on the fringes of the congregation. Still, in a culture that prizes efficiency over relationship enough to ensure self-checkout lanes in every store, it is worth asking whether we have imbibed some of these tendencies in our churches.

- Do our ministry programs funnel people into discipleship relationships or help them check boxes as they track their program progress?

- Do our ministry structures resemble assembly lines or do they have the flexibility to respond to the needs each person has as they grow in their discipleship?
- Do we measure success merely by assessing program participation or by intentionally observing ways people are demonstrating growth in Christ and Christlikeness?
- Do our efforts to expand our ministry reach sacrifice our capacity to know and invest in the individuals entrusted to us here and now?

If our goal in ministry is conditioned by the abiding desire to see the gospel transform lives, then we must be committed to making sure we are regularly in the lives of those around us. As we don our missionary glasses, we are reminded afresh that ministry is about people growing in their love and knowledge of the Lord. If our structures separate ministers from people, those structures are not worth keeping regardless of how efficient they are. We don't disciple numbers; we disciple people.

Serving Christ's Kingdom Out of Gospel Gratitude

A second way Newbigin challenges American ministry models is by his example of a lifelong gratitude for his own conversion. As we have already seen, Newbigin was a giant of a figure in twentieth-century missions, missiology, and global Christianity. He was in demand as a speaker, influential as a church leader, and was the catalyst of broad gospel impact in India and around the world. An outside observer of his accolades and influence could justifiably identify Newbigin as a ministry celebrity.

Yet while he had the admiration of many, Newbigin resisted the temptation to embrace his fame by maintaining a consistent amazement at the goodness of God to save and use a wretch like himself. Despite opportunity to think highly of himself, he remained humbled to be a servant and messenger of the undeserved grace by which he was being saved.

If you have been in a season of fruitfulness in ministry, it is easy to begin to believe you are a key part of the success equation. In fact, there may be many people who would come to you and tell you that very thing. They might not come out and say it as bluntly as this, but when they ask you to speak, they are implying you have something unique to say. When they ask you to write, they are indicating your words bear unique value. And when they seek you out for your advice, they are telling you that you offer special wisdom.

But again, the national stages and book contracts are not the only means by which people can awaken the ego of a minister. The same whispers that stroke a pastor's ego by highlighting his contribution can be communicated by much more common means. And the rush of endorphins that comes with being affirmed can deform a person's ministry into an insatiable search for recognition.

These are the places I found myself tempted upon my return from the mission field. Where Muslims didn't usually care what I had to say about the gospel, Christians at home sought me out to tell them how to talk to their Muslim friends. Where my Twitter account was used for maintaining safety while I was abroad, I discovered the pleasure of having a handful of people I've never met affirm some thought I posted with a simple click.

Whether you are a pastor of a mega church or a volunteer in the children's ministry, there are countless opportunities, both big and small, for you to be noticed for your contributions. Though it is right and good for believers to express appreciation for one another's labor in the gospel, it opens the door for all of us to begin thinking more highly of ourselves and our contributions than we ought. And worse, the desire for further affirmation and broader appreciation of our efforts can actually shape and distort our future ministry.

Much to my embarrassment now, I remember some of the things that went through my head as I was shooting baskets in my backyard alone as a kid. Though it would have been far better for my game to work on my free-throws (a perpetual weakness), I spent hours throwing up what I imagined to be buzzer-beating fade-away shots from deep in the back corner of the slab. As I watched each shot from the ground, having tripped backwards over the picnic table in the process, I also imagined Phil Jackson—then coach of the Chicago Bulls—driving through our alleyway by chance and seeing my flashy moves. Surely he would notice my unique skill, appreciate my potential as a forward despite my sixth-grade gangly frame, and offer me a contract then and there.

Most of us will at various times face the temptation to be noticed so that we might be given a chance to display our gifts on a bigger stage. But ministry—like basketball—is fundamentally about the fundamentals. Flashy gimmicks and pithy platitudes might attract attention to ourselves, but they distract from the ministry of the gospel. As we don our missionary lenses and seek to minister out of a fresh awe at our own salvation, there are a few more diagnostic questions we might ask to inspect our own ministries and hearts:

- Does knowing that my sermon will be available to an online audience distract me from preaching to the specific congregation entrusted to me?
- Does being affirmed in a certain aspect of ministry dissuade me from investing in and developing others in this area for fear of being overshadowed?
- Do I find myself planning and strategizing in order to be noticed by someone of influence?
- Do I minister out of a desire for the people in front of me to encounter the awe of the gospel, or do I want my audience to walk away in awe of my ministry?

It is truly the Lord's kind grace to use his people as jars of clay through which he conveys his surpassing glory. But it is always important to remember that the vessel does not produce the glory it possesses. Unfortunately, as sinful humans, we are well-versed in taking the credit for the glorious work God has done through us.

Whether you speak regularly to an audience of thousands or whether your mom is the only one who likes your Instagram posts, you are unnecessary to God's kingdom. It is only his kindness that invites you to have any part—big or small—in what he is doing.

As a missionary, Newbigin was aware he was indebted to the gospel. He was likewise compelled into all he did by the unshakable appreciation for the gospel he knew he didn't deserve. Rediscovering this same gratitude for the gospel will save us from clamoring for a bigger platform at the expense of faithfully ministering the gospel to those entrusted to us. And this brings us to the final challenge: investing in the church.

Invest in the Church as the Body of Christ

Third, Newbigin's insistence that local churches are the means of God's kingdom expansion presents a challenge to trends within American evangelicalism. Of course, Newbigin was not averse to working outside of the church. He spent seasons of ministry in theological education and invested in parachurch networks, such as the World Council of Churches. Yet despite seeing value in these parachurch ministries, Newbigin remained committed to the local church as the key to equipping the saints to live out the gospel in and for the place the Lord has put them.

We should pause here and ask whether American evangelicalism exhibits the same conviction about the church.

In the last several decades, networks of ever-more-specialized parachurch ministries have multiplied. These networks are usually formed by gathering people around specific shared affinities and areas of particular concern. We have parachurch college ministries and sports ministries. We see coalitions of believers dedicated to defending particular understandings of biblical anthropology or the relation of faith to science. Other groups form to promote specific methods and styles of preaching, counseling, evangelism, and church planting. Christian motorcycle enthusiasts even have their own network of bikers! The list goes on and on.

Since the internet and national conference culture allows such groups to avoid being restricted to a particular geographic location, people from various local churches can participate in and associate with these networks. There is an undeniable advantage to being able to benefit from the insight and reflection of experts who have demonstrated success in a niche area of ministry. But the danger is that the singularity of focus can at times lead to placing disproportionate value on these individual interests.

Think of it this way. My mom loves petunias. When springtime thaw allows a spade to break through the frozen Wisconsin tundra, it delights her heart to plant a tray of petunias in the flower bed out back. But if my mom filled the whole backyard with petunias, the yard would no longer provide an environment for all the activities that the family uses the backyard for.

Now, my mom would not say that the importance of her petunias is somehow diminished by denying them the exclusive right of place in the backyard. That is because she recognizes the yard is for the diverse purposes of the whole family. Her petunias complement my basketball court, my dad's manicured lawn, and my sister's picnic tea parties.

In the same way as the yard is for more than petunias, so too is the ministry of the church more than a handful of contemporary special interests. None of the narrowly focused parachurch networks can fulfill the multipurpose missional task that is entrusted to the church. Parachurch ministries can support the church, but they must not be allowed to supplant the church.

Some church members are drawn to associate with these networks independently of their churches. If their local church does not treat this particular issue with the same gravity as the network assigns it, they may be tempted to leave the church over a preference issue. Over time, they can begin to identify more as a disciple of the network than as a disciple of the church.

Pastors and ministry leaders who are concerned with these specific issues likewise face unique temptations in light of these supplementary ministries. On one hand, the allure of gaining a voice within this particular circle can draw them to invest more in securing their place of influence within their tribe than in affecting holistic gospel change with and through their church. On the other hand, their interest in a niche area of ministry or theology can cause them to lead the church to be known more for its stance on this issue than for ministering the whole gospel to the whole community.

As with the previous challenges, let me provide a few diagnostic questions that can help us investigate whether we are convinced the church is the answer or whether we are more confident that the future of the gospel hangs in the ministry of a particular network or coalition.

- Pastor, as you prepare your sermon, are you
  thinking of how this will help instruct your

congregation, or how to gain the approval of
your network of choice?

- Ministry leader, do you equip the saints
entrusted to you to apply the gospel in all
areas of their lives, or are you disproportion-
ately concerned with select areas?

- Christian, do you sit under the authority of
the Word preached in your church, or do
you scrutinize each message through the lens
of your coalition's priorities?

The temptation in a world of increasing specialization and
particularity is to let that mentality shape our view of ministry. In
reality, however, the church must extend beyond the niche interests we all have.

The ministry of the whole church to the whole place is not
accomplished merely by attending
to our own special interest issues.
Neither is it merely advanced by
professionals and specialists. The
kingdom of God advances as whole
churches of diversely gifted members are equipped by the whole
counsel of Scripture to minister
where the Lord has placed them.
The diversity of gifts, interests,
and vocations we bring into the
church gathering serves a missional

> **The kingdom of God advances as whole churches of diversely gifted members are equipped by the whole counsel of Scripture to minister where the Lord has placed them.**

purpose as the church scatters to the corners of the community where the members spend their week.

Using Our Yard for Ministry

For Lesslie Newbigin, the task of missions requires investment in local churches because this is God's "plan A" for advancing his purposes and kingdom on earth. As a missionary who wanted his investment to last long beyond his presence in a place, Newbigin poured himself into the local church. This is the arena for teaching the variously gifted members of Christ's body how to apply the whole counsel of Scripture to every corner of their lives.

Kingdom work is not merely the niche-work of attending to our pet issues. Nor is it the efficient assembly-line work of cleverly devised mass-ministry models. Kingdom work is church work. Church work occurs through the long, slow, investment of discipling the people in your midst and in your life. This local, personal ministry of making and deploying disciples as disciple-makers may look slower and messier than giving a well-crafted address to thousands at a conference or writing blogs that could reach millions. But Jesus says it is his church—not our conferences—that will overcome the gates of hell.

Like my childhood backyard, we are not primarily interested in producing manicured and marketable ministry models. Our task of making disciples requires us to be involved with people in the messiness of in-process lives. If we are truly seeking to leverage our lives for maximum kingdom impact, we must commit ourselves to allowing God's ways to take priority over ours—even when our ways promise to be more efficient or effective. His strategy for kingdom growth is his church. The church is the living household of God, the pillar and buttress of the truth as it is embodied, declared, and applied to all of life. So, let us use every avenue of ministry available to us, while also making certain that the only place we put our hope is in Christ and his bride.

Chapter 7

Our Address

Keeping Our Eyes on Our True Citizenship

On my first day of preschool at the YMCA, my teacher made me memorize my phone number and my address. If I ever got lost, I was instructed to find a police officer and tell them where I lived and how to contact my parents. The fearful possibility of getting lost coupled with the newly discovered academic pressure to perform caused me to burn that information indelibly into my young brain.

Because of that first day of preschool, I can still recite the address of that childhood home and I also know my first phone number by heart—including its original 414 area code that changed in grade school when our address was shifted over onto the 920 part of the grid.

By the time I returned home to get the house ready for sale, I had moved away to college and gotten my first cell phone, so my phone number had changed already. But 847 North 6th Street was still the home address I recorded on all my documents and in all of my official records. This address still represented home to me in many ways.

As I stood in the front yard and looked over the house just before getting in the car to leave for the last time, the sunlight glinting off the ceramic house numbers caught my eye. Three rectangular number plates cradled in a metal frame and held in place by two screws identified this house as my childhood home.

A knot formed in my throat, and I had to do everything I could to stop myself from running up to the front porch, unscrewing the plate, and keeping that placard as a reminder of home. I rationalized stealing away with this memento, thinking this address will always be mine. After all, it ties me to the place that provided so much of the influential environment of my youth.

But quickly on the heels of this rationalization I realized these numbers no longer represented my home. While I am grateful for the formation that took place at this address, home was somewhere else. More importantly, taking this address with me would only encourage me to try to find home in an old address rather than finding home where I lived now.

As I pulled away from that familiar address, the house in the rearview was familiar, but it was no longer my home. And as I wiped a stray tear from the corner of my eye, I reminded myself that home is a better name for the place you *are*, rather than a name inextricably bound to where you were. It is better to hope for home ahead of you than to think of it as somewhere behind you. If home is a place in the past, you cannot ever really be at home in the present.

Our American Address: Political Kingdoms

In many ways, Christians are people with two homes. Or maybe, we could conceive of ourselves as those living as dual-citizens. Each of us has been granted an earthly citizenship on the basis of the family, location, and details of our birth. But beyond this, God has granted us citizenship from heaven and promised us a coming heavenly home. Unfortunately, it seems that American evangelicals have too often experienced citizenship confusion.

What I mean by this is that we have at times given our earthly citizenship priority. We have asked our nation and our politics to provide and support our heavenly citizenship. In many ways, the wrestling with finding my sense of home in an old street address I described above serves as an analogy for the American evangelical church. We need to discern what it means to give allegiance to our heavenly citizenship as our primary home.

To do so, we might ask some reflective questions of ourselves:

- Is my home allegiance tied to the address stamped in my passport, or is it bound up in the irrevocable citizenship that will come with the arrival of my heavenly home?
- Which home address do I functionally place my hopes in and shape my life by?
- Do I feel more kinship with those who share my earthly citizenship or heavenly citizenship?

- Do I find myself predicting either doom or
  paradise when waiting to see the outcome of
  elections or supreme court decisions?
- Is a political loss devastating? Is a political
  victory euphoric?
- Do I worry that an election or a court decision will be the end of the church in America?

Ultimately in this chapter I want to prompt us to wrestle
with this question: Do we function primarily as citizens of earthly
kingdoms that promise to establish heaven on earth? Or do we
associate ourselves primarily with the heavenly kingdom that
promises to restore earth?

Recent American History and the Church

It is no secret that the American political landscape is increasingly polarized. Pundits and cultural commentators have pointed
to 2016 as a watershed year in which people began to race toward
the extremes. Conservative circles are spawning ever-more right-
wing extremist groups who espouse conspiracy theories and dangerous anti-social attitudes. Liberal-leaning circles feature fringe
groups that are pushing progressive ideologies so far beyond the
pale of reason that it would be humorous if they were not serious
and influential.

In the current American environment, it seems as though
everything has become politicized and, thereby, has become
volatile. Evangelical Christians have at times split publicly over

COVID vaccines and protocols, over how to address racial tensions in the nation, and how we are to respond to immigrants and refugees in our midst. In a cultural context that draws people into political alliances according to preset policy positions, these split opinions have at times pitted Christians against one another in the political sphere as well as within the church.

Jesus said in John 13:35 that the world would know we are his disciples by our love for one another. A few chapters later, in John 17, Jesus also prayed that we would be united by his word as a testimony to the gospel for the world to see. If a loving unity is to be regained despite political differences, American evangelicals must reconsider where we find our primary citizenship.

This entanglement with politics is not, however, a recent development. Long before things became so polarized and extreme, many of us evangelicals had already been investing our hopes in earthly kingdoms that promised to help establish Jesus's kingdom. A clear example of this might be seen in folks like Jerry Falwell and his Moral Majority efforts to lobby for political changes that would legislate Christian values. But less formalized versions work their way into churches around specific policies or candidates that are marketed as end-of-the-world issues as well.

Now, American Christians should be engaged in politics, and should be voting according to their Christian values. However, the often-unseen danger is the slow slide toward placing our hopes in legislative power to bring about a Christian society. And just like any other means that we try to justify by noble ends, our attempt to welcome the kingdom via political mechanisms all too often undermines our ability to see the world through the lens of the gospel.

Newbigin's Missionary Perspective: Keep Kingdom Citizenship Primary

During the early years of Newbigin's ministry, India was functionally under British rule. While World War I had shaken the confidence of some who anticipated technology and modernity to usher in a new age of human flourishing, Britain—and the British church—still operated as if the civilization they were bringing to India was the key to India's development, maturity, and prosperity. During the second decade of Newbigin's missionary career, World War II, the Holocaust, and the rejection of paternalistic colonialism further dampened the optimism that Western governance and economic development were what India needed.

Despite losing confidence that imposing British civilization would lead to an Indian utopia, back home in England the political promises continued to be issued. Newbigin discovered differing visions of progress and political persuasions divided people inside the church and outside of the church. Having seen governance in various places around the world, Newbigin was able to provide a clear warning that governments and politicians will always promise more than they can deliver.

> **Governments and politicians will always promise more than they can deliver.**

156

And furthermore, their promises and methods always pale in comparison to the assured victory that comes by alliance with the kingdom of heaven.

Newbigin was neither an anarchist nor was he antiauthoritarian. He was, however, keen to call the church to a proper confidence in the unshakable kingdom of their primary citizenship. I want to briefly highlight five ways he helps us to see the relationship between the church and politics, politicians, governments, and nations through missionary lenses. Each of these five steps is important to helping the church restore a lived-out confidence in the promises of the gospel without relying on the kings and kingdoms of the world for help.

1. See the Lesser Power of Worldly Ways

The first way Newbigin calls the church to live as citizens of the heavenly kingdom is by pointing out the lesser nature of the power offered by the world. For example, in *The Gospel in a Pluralist Society*, Newbigin reminds his readers that the martyrs of the early church demonstrated their primary allegiance to Christ's kingdom in the face of the Roman government that persecuted them for their faith. Urging his audience to take the same posture, Newbigin writes, "The victory of the Church over the demonic power which was embodied in the Roman imperial system was not won by seizing the levers of power: it was won when the victims knelt down in the Colosseum and prayed in the name of Jesus for the Emperor."[1]

He goes on in this same passage to recognize that, as these martyrs lived out their confidence in the power of the gospel, they exposed the weakness of the world's power, promises, and story. He writes,

> The soldiers in Christ's victorious army were not armed with the weapons of this age; they were the martyrs whose robes were washed in blood. It was not that a particular Emperor was discredited and displaced; it was that the entire mystique of the Empire, its spiritual power, was unmasked, disarmed, and rendered powerless. A conversion of individuals which failed to identify, unmask, and reject that spiritual, ideological power would have been as futile as an attempt by Christians to wrest that power from its holders.[2]

Now, we may bristle at the idea of identifying politicians and politics with demonic forces and spiritual powers. Certainly, this language has been wielded poorly at various times, and it is right to be cautious about such labeling. But Newbigin's point was not to associate his political opponents with the kingdom of darkness.

---

1. Lesslie Newbigin, *The Gospel in a Pluralist Society* (Grand Rapids: Eerdmans, 1989), 210.

2. Newbigin, *The Gospel in a Pluralist Society*, 210.

Rather, Newbigin urges us to see that whenever we are tempted to give our allegiance to worldly methods, means, and mechanisms in order to gain what can only come through the power of King Jesus and his gospel, we are colluding with a rival kingdom. Any time we find ourselves trusting legislation more than providence, we are in danger of confusing kingdoms. Likewise, when we find ourselves fearing an election or a controversial issue could undermine the church, it should cause us to ask which kingdom we are placing our hope in.

Having issued this warning against buying into the promises offered through worldly power, Newbigin provides positive ways of developing a Christian perspective on how to be a citizen and participant in worldly politics. He begins with a reminder of where our home is and how essential it is to remember our true address while living among the kingdoms of the world.

2. Affirm the Unshakable Foundation

Newbigin's missionary mindset reminds us that, as those who long to proclaim the gospel to the lost, engagement with the world is part of our Christian duty. In the American political system, where citizens are expected to participate in the governance, political involvement is both a necessity and a responsibility for Christians. Churches must train their members to participate in the public arena from a firm and unshakable foundation of biblical truth and hope. Christians enter the political arena making affirmations of what is ultimate in the world.

For Newbigin, then, while the church must resist unchecked affiliation with any particular party, this does not mean she should be apolitical. In fact, his second piece of advice to churches caught between political triumphalism and passivity comes as he writes,

> The Church is not to identify itself with any particular political program, and yet cannot leave political issues out of her concern, as though the sovereignty of Christ did not extend beyond the walls of the church. . . . The first duty [of the church in the political realm] is affirmation. The Church must affirm the truth of the gospel, the fact of the sovereignty of Christ as sole Lord and Savior, and the Trinitarian faith, the given starting point, the dogma which must shape all our thinking and revising. To affirm this in season and out of season, whether they hear or refuse to hear, is in fact the most radical political action that we can take.[3]

Therefore, as Newbigin discusses the relationship between the kingdom of heaven and the kingdom of this world, he sees the gospel as an explicitly political claim. As we affirm Jesus as the sole and sovereign king, we subject any and all political rulers and nations to his authority.

---

3. Lesslie Newbigin, *Truth to Tell: The Gospel as Public Truth* (Grand Rapids: Eerdmans, 1991), 79–80.

Though this advice may seem as though it is either too obvious for a Christian to bother reading or too esoteric to be implemented, it is the key starting place that cannot be overlooked. But where we are called to make affirmations, Newbigin notes that we are also called to the task of issuing anathemas.[4]

3. Reject the "Secular" Absolutization of Lesser Things

The United States was built upon the commitment that people should have the freedom to practice their faith freely and without compulsion from the state. As long as the church—the sacred realm of religion—and the state—the secular realm of human governance—stay in their respective lanes, they can and should coexist in relative peace. These two entities often function according to a kind of truce where the church will agree not to impose its beliefs on the state if the state will not attempt to impose its authority on the church.

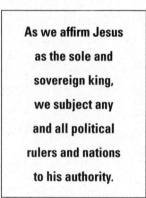

As we affirm Jesus as the sole and sovereign king, we subject any and all political rulers and nations to his authority.

Christians have often agreed to this truce to protect their freedom of worship, noting that secular, human governments are endorsed in the Bible as God-given means for governing human affairs and relationships. The problem is the state often takes such

---

4. Newbigin, *Truth to Tell*, 80–81.

a concession to mean it can, within the realm of state matters, demand the absolute allegiance of its citizens.

The problem that Newbigin notes in this tenuous truce, however, is the church is not of a kingdom that is merely adjacent to the kingdoms of this world. The church is of a king and a kingdom that lays claim to having absolute authority over every realm. By conceding the task of human governance to the realm of the secular state, the church has at times abdicated her right to speak prophetically into the so-called secular affairs in order to limit herself to sacred concerns.

If Jesus's kingdom reign extends over everything, then, as ambassadors of his kingdom, the church must be ready to challenge the leaders of the state when they over-promise or assert a sovereignty that belongs to Christ alone. No nation can demand absolute allegiance to the state because no nation can provide the salvation and citizenship that comes from Christ's kingdom. Newbigin puts it this way as he offers a third piece of advice to the church in the world:

> With affirmation there has to be anathema. We have to reject ideologies which give to particular elements in God's ordering of things the central and absolute place which belongs to Christ alone. It is good to love and serve the nation in which God has set us; we need more, not less

true patriotism. But to give absolute commitment to the nation is to go into bondage.[5]

In other words, we do not just affirm Jesus as Lord of the
sacred at the same time as our politicians and nations affirm
themselves as lords of the secular. We must regularly say to our
church members and to the watching world that the only absolute
authority belongs to God. Thus, our allegiance is his alone.

Such a posture—even in a society that tries to keep a divide
between church and state—will inevitably bring about conflict
between the faithful within the church and those in politics who
seek to expand their own power. While previous generations of
American evangelicals could count on the broader world to have
a generally favorable disposition toward them and their faith, this
is no longer the case. Thus, Newbigin's fourth piece of advice calls
church leaders to train church members to keep Christ as Lord in
their engagements in the public square.

4. Inform, Train, and Deploy Church Members

As I observed above, the American cultural landscape has
changed dramatically in the past fifty years. Once given a defer-
ential respect by those outside the church, evangelicals are today
often received with scorn or disdain. While many of our fore-
bearers expected to effect social changes through their efforts as

---

5. Newbigin, *Truth to Tell*, 80.

political lobbyists, the influence that was sought through these channels has proven evasive and at times corrupting.

With this reality in front of us, we must no longer speak to politics as insider lobbyists who can count on having influence. We must instead take the posture of prophets speaking to power on both sides of the aisle from the outside. Newbigin helps with this as he offers three suggestions for the preparation of the church for public engagement.

First, *Newbigin notes that 1 Peter 2:9–10 speaks of believers as being part of a royal priesthood.* He notes that priests are those tasked with interceding between God and people—representing people before their God and representing God to his people. Leaning into this priestly language, Newbigin urges church leaders to equip church members in the church's gathering for the priestly tasks they will encounter as they scatter. He writes, "The Church gathers on the Lord's Day to renew the priesthood by renewing its incorporation in the one High Priest. It should become part of the normal work of the Church to equip its members for the exercise of this priesthood in the many different areas of secular life."[6]

Second, *since withdrawal is not an option for the missional church, Newbigin encourages some Christians to seek public office.* He envisions a convictional engagement with public life as he writes, "If we accept the model of what I have called a committed pluralism, we can look for and work for a time when Christian leadership (not Christian domination) can shape society, shape

---

6. Newbigin, *Truth to Tell*, 84.

the plausibility structure [or worldview] within which people make their decisions and come to their beliefs."[7] Christian politicians must fight against the temptation to pursue political power in order to dominate the public sphere by demanding conformity to a Christian agenda.

Despite the temptation to dominance, Newbigin urges the church to encourage some of its members to take on Christlike leadership in the public square. He envisions Christian politicians who would lead from a convictional and yet uncoercive posture as Jesus did, writing, "The remedy is not to deny the necessity for leadership; that is simply evasion. It is the summons to a leadership which is modeled on that of the one whose words 'Follow me' are constitutive of the church."[8] The church does well, then, to intentionally develop the theology and convictions of its members who are tasked with serving as Christian leaders in the public square.

But for Newbigin, this task does not merely fall to the church leadership and those the church commissions into political leadership. His third suggestion is *to call the whole church to display allegiance to Christ's kingdom.* The church must do so in their regular gathering and in their scattering. The ministry of testifying to a more stable kingdom than the ones on offer from the world is an every-member ministry. And it brings us to Newbigin's fifth contribution to our thinking missionally about politics.

---

7. Newbigin, *Truth to Tell*, 85.
8. Newbigin, *Truth to Tell*, 85.

5. *Live Out the Hope of the Better Story*

One of Newbigin's repeated claims in his writing is that publicly living out our confidence in Christ's lordship is the most consistent way the church can demonstrate the beauty of his radical kingdom. But to live this out, we must not demonstrate our willingness to divide among one another on the basis of our political opinions. If American politics belong to a lower kingdom, why would we so quickly sacrifice the unity of the church for them?

And yet this has been the heartbreaking pattern that we in the American church have followed with increasing frequency over the last several years. This is not to imply there are not serious concerns that might be part of an underlying cause of division that runs deeper than politics. However, I have in mind the divisive and highly politicized tirades that have split fellowships over trivial matters such as mask mandates during the COVID-19 pandemic or whether or not an election was fair. For some, these issues may not feel trivial. But step back for a second and think with the apostle Paul about the contrast between these light and momentary trials—trials that for Paul included actual persecution—with the glory of eternity. These are not issues that should be allowed to divide the bride.

From an onlooker's perspective, it may seem as though we claim Jesus is Lord of an unshakable and eternal kingdom only to functionally deny this confidence by our divisiveness. By accusing other Christians of contributing to the demise of the church due to their differing political priorities, we demonstrate that we trust politics to uphold the church more than we trust the message of the church to confront and dethrone the false kings across the political spectrum.

As Newbigin surveyed the relationship between churchmen and politics in his day, he saw many believers who allowed their zeal for particular moral issues to distract from their commitment to living out the gospel holistically and in relationship to their brothers and sisters in Christ. He writes of this phenomenon incisively in his book *Truth to Tell*:

> It *is* the case that many Christians have a rather tepid faith in this fundamental dogma [the truth of the gospel, the sovereignty of Christ as sole Lord and Savior, and the Trinitarian faith] and therefore tend to invest the zeal and the commitment which are properly owed to it in particular moral and political causes. We get the widespread phenomenon of single-issue Christians, Christians for whom the whole of Christianity is equated with support for a particular cause and the Church is valued only as it supports that cause. Moral and political commitments which are legitimate implications of the Christian faith in a particular situation are allowed to displace the fundamental dogma. And it follows, of course, that those who regard other issues as the urgent ones for here and now are effectively excommunicated. Once again, that which

is good and proper at its own level is corrupted
when it is absolutized.[9]

As I read this passage, I cannot help but think of the divisive
and dismissive rhetoric that accompanies our public display of the
political opinions we have absolutized.

Specifically, I think of the occasions that I've seen and heard
statements that begin with, "You cannot be a Christian and vote
for (fill in the blank)." Or, "Anyone who supports (fill in the
blank) has compromised the gospel." Or, "If you align with (fill
in the blank), you are to blame for the death of the church in
America."

Brothers and sisters, there must be a better way for Christians
to differ over the lesser-kingdom things than what we have been
doing. Let us have disagreements and let us hold different opinions. But let us engage with one another over these differences
with a charity befitting of family and with confidence that we
stand together on a shared and unshakable foundation! When
Christians accuse one another of holding political opinions that
will undermine the church, it publicly undermines our claim that
God is sovereign and no political power can topple his church.

As we consider what it might look like to prioritize our citizenship in Christ's kingdom, these five pieces of advice helpfully
remind us to remember our heavenly home address. However,
I would like to add one more of my own, because we have not
yet noted that the church in America is itself part of the global

---

9. Newbigin, *Truth to Tell*, 80.

church. It is not just our politics but also our nationalism that can get in the way of our missional task of displaying the gospel to those around us. Let me start with a story from our return from the mission field.

The American Church vs. the Church in America

Within a few weeks of stepping off the plane, I found myself in a local high school gymnasium on a Sunday morning for a community church service. Several of the area churches had a habit of gathering together once or twice a year in order to celebrate our common faith in Jesus as a broader multi-denominational community. I was initially thrilled with the prospect of a community-wide gathering of believers whose denominational and doctrinal commitments kept them from gathering with one another weekly, but whose shared commitment to the gospel of Jesus could be celebrated nonetheless.

Upon arriving, however, I found myself growing increasingly uncomfortable. The gymnasium was adorned with the emblems of various branches of the military and posters depicting the stars and stripes of the United States of America. I dismissed the décor, thinking that perhaps these were school-related and could have been hung by students during their American history classes. But as I took my seat, I quickly noticed the loudspeakers were piping in various patriotic songs. It was Labor Day, so I excused it initially as a nod to our gratitude for the freedom to worship unmolested granted to us by our nation. But once the speaker took the stage, standing alongside of an American flag that had been posted immediately adjacent to the podium, I realized this entire event was being intentionally cloaked in the banner of American pride.

The speaker for the day began his address saying, "I have a lot to tell you today, but the most important thing you'll hear from me is this: pray every day, read your Bible, and be at church on Sundays." These three injunctions are good advice, of course, but there was nothing in what followed that could have been connected to these three application points. In fact, the forty minutes following this opening sentence were filled with stories of the speaker's experiences in war, punctuated with stories in which the American military saw unlikely victories over their adversaries in places like Japan and southeast Asia.

As I scanned the room, praying I would not find any of our Asian American neighbors in attendance, I found myself observing swaths of people who didn't seem to be confused about what was happening. People were nodding along. They were nudging their neighbors and whispering corroborating accounts from their own experiences in the military. And everyone lined up afterward, excited to shake hands with the man who had used the hour of community church to tell about the strength of the American Army. I walked out wondering if it was too late to get back on a plane to North Africa.

This was a definite case of reverse-culture-shock.

But rather than move on from it, growing accustomed to the marriage between patriotism and church, I want to drill into this discomfort in order to investigate whether or not this may be a point at which some within the American church can be dabbling with syncretism. At the very least, I believe we have been tempted to conflate our allegiance to Christ with our possession of American citizenship in ways that make the gospel of the kingdom subservient to the prosperity of the nation.

One recent exhibition of this took place on January 6, 2021. I was in my office, preparing for the upcoming semester, when one of my colleagues texted me and said, "There are people taking over the Capitol building!" Not having a TV nearby, I opened up my Twitter account to find scads of videos, pictures, and initial reports of the pro-Trump protestors who had stormed the Capitol grounds and interrupted the ratification of the election of President Biden. The most

> **We have been tempted to conflate our allegiance to Christ with our possession of American citizenship.**

disturbing part of watching these events unfold, however, had nothing to do with the facile attempt to interrupt the democratic process, but the numerous images of Christian symbols being used to baptize the actions of the demonstrators.

There were pictures of people holding signs that said, "Jesus Saves" as they broke down doors and forcefully entered the buildings. There were images of people circling together in prayer while donning protective gear in preparation for the chaos they intended to generate. And perhaps most vile of all, I saw images of people wearing "Trump: Make America Great Again" flags like a cape as they bowed a knee of allegiance to a homemade cross.

An outside observer might be excused for wondering what connection exists between the central symbol of Christian hope and a one-term president being denied reelection. But January 6th is not as anomalous as it might have seemed to those watching it unfold. If we have become accustomed to conflating American politics with our Christian faith, as seen in the Labor Day community service described above, storming the Capitol in the name of Jesus and for the "Christian" candidate is nothing more than Christian duty. But as we are instructed not to take the name of the Lord in vain, we must not use the name of the Lord to consecrate our vanities.

Politics, Nationalism, and the Church through Missionary Lenses

You may read this chapter and find my reaction to be overblown or inappropriately antagonistic toward Christian engagement in politics. A single anecdote about a well-meaning gathering of Christians in a Midwestern town does not lead automatically to an attempted coup in the name of Christ. And if a few war stories told by an elderly war vet are enough to offend a visitor, perhaps they need to grow some thicker skin.

Perhaps you might accuse me of advocating for an approach to politics that will slowly erode our collective resolve to fight various social evils. Or perhaps your concerns might be that this approach to politics leads to a passivity that will discourage the church from working to dismantle imbalanced power structures in society.

If any of this is your fear, I would encourage you to take up the challenge of Newbigin's fourth piece of advice above: *engage in the public square boldly and as a Christian whose confidence is squarely grounded in the kingdom where your citizenship unshakably rests.* Advocate for your convictions within the church. Mobilize the church to speak—not on behalf of a political party, but from the convictions we have in the gospel to address both abortion and injustice, along with a myriad of other concerns held by various political parties.

I do not in any way want people to cease being appropriately patriotic, nor do I want to discourage Christian engagement in the political arena. The point I really intend to get across in this chapter is that many of us have been making little compromises with worldly kings and kingdoms that have radically reshaped the way we think about our place in society and about the demands of the gospel. These compromises have at times corrupted our vision of the church as a mission station or an outpost of the kingdom of heaven. We may not be in the crowds that were storming the Capitol building, but without noticing it, we may find that we have begun looking at the gospel and the Christian life through the lens of our earthly political preferences.

Gospel Lenses or Political Lenses: Self-Reflection and Self-Assessment

Recently, I had a scare with my eyesight. My vision in one eye got blurry right at the center. As it turned out, there was a small chip in the lens of my glasses that was distorting my vision.

Everything I saw through those lenses was distorted, so I needed to stop looking through them and first look at them to find the problem.

Just like the lenses in a pair of eyeglasses, our American political sensibilities often function like the lenses through which we view the world. As Christians, then, we must always be inspecting whether our primary lenses are gospel lenses or party lenses.

Let me illustrate how to do this with a lens-inspection exercise. Consider your response to the following opinions:

- If I speak positively about welcoming refugees and immigrants and about the need for immigration reform, is your first thought that I lean left politically?
- If I speak out against the injustice of killing children in utero and cheer Supreme Court decisions to limit and outlaw abortion, do you assume my politics lean right?
- If I hold these two opinions at the same time, do you sense an incompatible tension? Do you find yourself viewing me as inconsistent?

Despite being in tension with the artificial political binary we perceive in the American public square, I believe these opinions are completely compatible within Jesus's kingdom. His desire to redeem and restore humanity in the gospel leads Christians to value life in the womb and at the border. But the reflex to view issues first through the lens of which political party the opinion aligns with is deeply ingrained in us as Americans, and even as American evangelicals.[10]

We have bought the lie that politicians can help us legislate the kingdom of God into being. In so doing, we have at times abdicated our gospel responsibility to speak prophetically from within the kingdom of God and into the kingdom of the world. We have avoided speaking against our preferred party for fear of losing a place of perceived influence with those we see as influential. In the end, we have often believed the kings of the world are on our team even though they are driven more by dollars and lobbyists than by the kingdom of God and his Word.

We have given ourselves over to the stories politicians tell, siding with them as the good guys to make sure the bad guys don't gain power. We have often had to rationalize our allegiance by over-emphasizing the importance of one issue or another in order to justify the elements of the party line that diverged from kingdom principles.

On the right, the hope of turning back abortion laws is rightly lauded as a worthy reason to endorse Republican candidates. Yet

---

10. Again here I would commend the insightful assessment of Carl Trueman, *The Rise and Triumph of the Modern Self: Cultural Amnesia, Expressive Individualism, and the Road to Sexual Revolution* (Wheaton, IL: Crossway, 2020), 334–35, "Unfortunately, once one side in the political debate chooses to politicize an issue, then all sides have to play that game. And the radical individualism of the libertarian Right, as much as the Marxist communitarianism of the Left, tends in this direction, because any corralling of individual behavior can be seen as a political assault on personal sovereignty. The truth is, we now live in a world in which everything is politicized, and we have no choice in the public square but to accept this and engage accordingly."

when immigration policies result in children being separated from their parents in detention facilities at the border, Christians face the tension of upholding a party line or speaking out prophetically against practices that are more interested in national security than human decency.

On the left, compassion for the poor and the marginalized highlights a biblical disposition and concern and gives reason to endorse Democratic candidates. But when religious liberty cases threaten to force people to affirm or participate in activities that violate their conscience, one faces the need to rationalize away the infringement on kingdom living.

The list of such tensions goes on and on. And while Christians who identify themselves as Republicans and Democrats will provide rationale for each of these issues, the fact of the tension should alert us to the fact that the two-party system into which we commonly divide is not equated with the kingdom of God. If Jesus is our king, he demands we be attentive to issues that either party would downplay.

The Incompatibility of Nationalism and Missions

In addition to the internal political divisions that threaten to divide churches, if we are wearing our missionary lenses we cannot overlook the way American nationalism can undermine the global nature of Christ's kingdom.

When we define American military or economic victory as God's blessing, we imply that those nations who are defeated or who lag behind are experiencing God's curse. If blessing is measured by these metrics, we begin to assess our favor in the eyes of the Lord on the basis of our increased GDP rather than on the basis of being in Christ. In so doing, we imply that our brothers and sisters who share in Christ but who are citizens of countries that lag behind America are somehow less blessed than we are. This, of course, ignores Jesus's teaching in the Beatitudes wherein blessing is measured by a very different standard.

Perhaps even more worrisome, though, is the celebration of American military exploits in the context of church services. As I described in the story above, war stories of American victory told in church services don't take into account the likelihood that citizens of nations with whom America has been at war may be present.

Perhaps it might help us to think through some self-reflection questions here again. For instance, you might ask yourself, your leadership team, or your congregation to put themselves in the following scenarios and consider their response:

- You are attending a Vietnamese church service. In the service the speaker regales the audience with stories of how he and his troop fought and sent the American military packing from Vietnam without victory. Would this amplify or distract from your participation in corporate worship?
- You are visiting a Russian church during a national holiday during which it is tradition for servicemen and servicewomen to worship

while dressed in their military uniforms as a way of recognizing them for their service. Does this amplify or distract from your participation in corporate worship?

- You are attending a church service in China. During the service, the congregation sings the Chinese national anthem and displays the Chinese flag. Would you be likely to interpret these symbols as an appropriate sign of gratitude for the way the Lord has placed governors over them by his providence? Or would you conclude that they have sold out as they celebrate the Communist government?

- You are in Canada and are worshipping at a small First Nations church. During the service the speaker points out the offensiveness of Mount Rushmore, showing how it has indelibly etched the faces of oppressors onto the sacred territory belonging to the Lakota people. Does it distract you from worship to have the actions of your nation's forefathers and leaders called into question?

You may find yourself eluding a simple answer to these questions by shifting to which country is more right or wrong. For example, you might say, "Well of course the Chinese national anthem would be offensive to me, but the United States isn't a Communist nation!" If so, you're missing the point by putting this-worldly politics on par with the kingdom of God. The Great Commission is far more important than our national loyalties, and if the latter detracts from the former in our worship services, we need to reconsider some things.

Reflecting on these simple scenarios can help us recognize the power of symbols to influence our perception of what we are doing. When we mix the symbols of worldly powers with the gathering that is intended to celebrate King Jesus's ultimate power, we send mixed messages to one another. Worse yet, to those who are looking in from the outside, these symbols of earthly kingdoms may obscure the gospel of Christ's heavenly kingdom.

I want to reinforce that I am proud of and grateful for my American citizenship. The irony is not lost on me that I am allowed to criticize some of our nationalistic tendencies without fear of recourse as a freedom that is afforded to me by this very country. I do not want to dampen our appreciation for these freedoms or for our country any more than I want to encourage Christians to withdraw from politics. However, I do want to push us to make sure our politics and our patriotism are both subservient to our calling as citizens and ambassadors of a greater kingdom.

That kingdom is one that is coming and is certain. It is not going to be built by human hands nor will its foundations be laid by our political ingenuity. Therefore, we must be diligent in reminding ourselves and our people that any story whose hoped-for promises are created and limited to that which can be affected in history and by humans are lesser than what is promised by our victorious heavenly king. As I close this chapter, I want to again commend Newbigin's insight into the power of the stories we believe to be ultimate.

One of the things Newbigin observed about the power of story is that if a person tells a story in which their perspective is vindicated in history, it becomes inherently imperialistic. In 1992 he put it this way:

> We can point to one feature of our [biblical] story that is unique. All the other stories look to an end within history. They look to the intrahistorical triumph of their cause. They are therefore inherently imperialist. The Church has sometimes acted in precisely that imperialistic way, but that is to betray her gospel. What is unique about the Christian story is that its crucial turning point is the event of Calvary and Easter, when we learn that the triumph of God is an event beyond history that gives meaning to all history. This means we can always be at the same time realistic and hopeful. We can face, as Amos and Jeremiah did, the most shattering disaster for the visible cause of God, and yet continue to act in confident hope because we know that the real victory has already been won. Of course the story will always be treated with skepticism and disbelief. That has always been so. What can make it credible is the existence of communities of people, local congregations, who believe it, celebrate it, live by it,

and allow the Bible to shape the way they see the
world. And we need Christians who learn to see
the world through the spectacles of the Bible.[11]

If we are viewing the world—its power, its politics, and its
promises—through the lens of Scripture, we will recognize there
is no preference given to our nation over and against any other
nation. Likewise, we will recognize that, though we have responsibilities to engage politically as citizens, politicians cannot deliver
what is already irrevocably ours in the gospel.

While we should remain grateful for the freedoms afforded
us within this country, we must not forget that those freedoms—
given or withheld—are only offered by politicians who are operating in a lower kingdom. Even if those freedoms which we enjoy
were withdrawn, the church of King Jesus would continue. This
is something we see in the harshest dictatorships and under the
totalitarian regimes of places like China and North Korea. The
church and the gospel that forms the church goes on because
King Jesus is the one who offers the freedom to follow him, not
a government.

May it be that as the world watches us live this out, they see a
community of people who, like Abraham, are "looking forward to
the city that has foundations, whose architect and builder is God"
(Heb. 11:10). This kingdom's foundations are both firm and compelling to onlookers who have seen the empty promises of politics
and politicians. What the world needs to see is a community of

---

11. Lesslie Newbigin, *A Word in Season: Perspectives on Christian World
Missions* (Grand Rapids: Eerdmans, 1994), 204.

kingdom citizens whose hopes are unshakable and whose message is truly ultimate. Brothers and sisters, let us diligently remember our address and commit it to heart.

Conclusion

What Kind of House?

The Missionary Nature of the Church

As we draw this home-inspection to a close, I have a haunting feeling that if Lesslie Newbigin read this book he would correct my approach. As I have been introducing Newbigin's insights, I have presented it as if we are putting on some special missionary lenses in order to inspect different areas of the church. However, I think Newbigin would reject the implication that we can look at the church with some sort of optional and extraneous missionary perspective. I agree. One cannot look at the church from a missionary perspective any more than one can look at water from a wetness perspective. Mission is intrinsic to the church.

When Newbigin returned to England, he did not merely bring a missionary perspective—he was already convinced the church is essentially missionary in nature. This means we don't just consider the missionary angle on a church issue, but that every issue the church faces, it faces as a missionary community.

For Newbigin, the church exists as a signpost for the kingdom amidst the rival kingdoms of the world. We do not, then, merely look at the church from a missionary perspective as much as we are to see it as a missionary community.[1]

The church is always intended to be a community of people who are gathered together by the gospel, in covenant to one another, and for the announcement and display of the kingdom in a specific place. This means that every room of the house—the dining room, living room, bedroom, and yard—participates in this missionary vocation of the church.

Reading about a missionary church may seem as if it is just one more new approach to doing church—much like the seeker-sensitive approach, the simple church approach, or the contagious disciple-making approach. But for Newbigin, this is not a discussion of church model, but church nature.

> **Mission is intrinsic to the church.**

---

1. I prefer to typically reserve the word *missionary* for pioneering work of disciple-making and church planting where gospel-access is limited. However, even though he applies "missionary" in places that the gospel is readily available, Newbigin's point in describing the church as a missionary body is to argue that the church is always on mission. While I prefer to use different terminology, I affirm Newbigin's purpose. In his brief book *Trinitarian Doctrine for Today's Mission*, Newbigin defines his use of missionary this way: "Among those who have reflected about these matters, it becomes less and less possible to speak of the missionary task otherwise than as the embassage of the whole people of God to the whole world." Lesslie Newbigin, *Trinitarian Doctrine for Today's Mission* (Eugene, OR: Wipf & Stock, 1988), 12.

As we conclude this book, I want to press once again into the importance of Newbigin's insights for contemporary American evangelicalism. Beyond the specific areas of life and ministry we've investigated above, I hope we can catch a glimpse of the vision that Newbigin had as he sketched out his missionary ecclesiology. It begins with what Newbigin referred to as his "naughty question."

Newbigin's Naughty Question

In 1988, Lesslie Newbigin presented an essay entitled "On Being the Church for the World," in which he confesses to asking what he labeled a "naughty question." While visiting a church in Madras India, he recounted a conversation with some national pastors, writing, "In a meeting of the elders after the service I asked the naughty question, 'What is this church for?'"[2] Following their embarrassed silence, one of the elders apparently suggested that the church was to meet the needs of its members, to which Newbigin replied, "'Then it should be dissolved.' The Church does not exist for its members."[3]

This is a jarring response. One might be tempted to wonder if Newbigin was having a bad day, or if there was some external

---

2. Lesslie Newbigin, "On Being the Church for the World," 25–42 in *The Parish Church? Explorations in the Relationship of the Church and the World*, ed. Giles S. Ecclestone (Oxford, UK: Mowbray, 1988), 28. As cited in Paul Weston, ed., *Lesslie Newbigin: Missionary Theologian* (Grand Rapids: Eerdmans, 2006), 133.

3. Newbigin, "On Being the Church for the World," 28.

cause to this rash answer. Yet if we follow the thread of Newbigin's missional ecclesiology, it is in fact the natural conclusion to his thought.

In these last pages, then, let us consider what Newbigin means when he speaks of a missional ecclesiology. This will involve seeing the web of interrelated concepts Newbigin has woven together to guide the church toward uncovering her missionary nature. In his helpful synthesis of Newbigin's work, Michael Goheen proposes a fourfold dynamic of concepts that form the web of ideas driving this missional ecclesiology.[4] We'll briefly look at each one as we seek to understand how Newbigin conceives the missionary nature of the church before considering how that works out in American evangelicalism.

Gospel: Worship and Allegiance

The first element of Newbigin's missionary ecclesiology is the gospel. His claim, as we have seen in various ways throughout this book, is that the gospel is the center of universal history. It serves

---

4. Michael Goheen, *The Church and Its Vocation: Lesslie Newbigin's Missionary Ecclesiology* (Grand Rapids: Baker, 2018), 9. In the introduction to his book, Goheen defends this fourfold dynamic, presenting Newbigin's thought as a closely intertwined relationship between (1) the gospel as the center of history, (2) the story of the universe, (3) the church as a missional people, and (4) the church and its members having a missionary encounter with the world. The headings that follow in this section are drawn from Goheen's helpful synthesis of Newbigin's thought.

as the turning point of history and provides the lens by which the entire narrative is to be interpreted.[5]

The gospel of Jesus's life, death, resurrection, and ascension is the hinge on which history hangs between the sin-stained separation of humanity from God and Jesus's substitutionary provision of a way of reconciliation. Newbigin centered his teaching on calling people to faith in this gospel. He likewise persisted in discipling people in such a way as to live out the implications of this gospel in every sphere of life after they had believed.

For Newbigin, as for Jesus, those who have freely received this message should have the natural posture to invite others to see the world through its clarifying lens. In other words, those who embrace this gospel are made beneficiary-ambassadors of the inbreaking kingdom of God. This leads to the second element of missional ecclesiology.

Story: Caught Between Beginning and End

The second contribution of Newbigin's thought is related to the gospel in the way that the climax of a novel is related to the rest of the narrative. The gospel is the center of universal history. But it is a center that only makes sense within the context of the story that has already been told. This means the Old Testament prepares us for the gospel, and the New Testament instructs us on how we are to live in light of the gospel.

---

5. Such a claim can be easily reinforced through Jesus's own ministry as he walked the Emmaus road with his two disciples and opened their eyes to how the Scriptures pointed to him in Luke 24.

This storied world the Bible invites us into is not merely concerned with the arenas of life we deem to be religious. Rather, the biblical story is totalizing, laying claim to the right interpretation of where everything comes from, where it is going, and why it has value. Thus, as people who are drawn up into this story by way of believing the gospel, we are invited to inhabit the biblical story today in every corner of our lives.

Such a holistic task—the application and extension of the biblical story into the whole of life—is one that is complicated by the fall. As individuals seek to live out of the gospel, they do so in the company of believers. This company of believers is called to manifest the corporate life of individual, communal, and even cosmic restoration that has been affected by the gospel. The process of embodying this story is given specific biblical language: disciple-making.

Missional People: Making Disciples

Third, Newbigin recognizes that though this story has to do with cosmic history, it is also the particular story being embraced by a particular people. Furthermore, this story is being believed and embodied by individuals who comprise this people. Consequently, those who have received this story by faith, and who have focused their interpretation of the world through its lens, have been unified in the task of living out this gospel. The Bible calls this process *discipleship*.

At the core of its task, the church is about the work of developing disciples who will likewise take up the task of living out the gospel story in every arena of life. Of this holistic vision for the missionary impact of disciple-making, Goheen summarizes Newbigin's thoughts, writing, "The gospel is an invitation to believe, follow, love, and obey Jesus, and that means entry into his kingdom-community and costly participation in his comprehensive mission."[6] All of these verbs—and the reference to Jesus's comprehensive mission—push for a holistic vision of applying a gospel-clarified understanding of human purpose in every arena in which we find ourselves.

> **Disciples are those who seek to live out the kingdom of God in the community of other believers and amidst the rival kingdoms of the world.**

Disciples, then, are those who seek to live out the kingdom of God in the community of other believers and amidst the rival kingdoms of the world. This results in a community that is embodying ultimate truth claims that conflict with the ultimate truth claims of those in the world. Thus, Newbigin's fourth mark of his missional ecclesiology focuses on the inevitability of a missionary encounter with the world.

---

6. Goheen, *The Church and Its Vocation*, 36.

Missionary Encounter with the World: Displaying the Kingdom

None of the practice of this faith happens in a vacuum. The gospel as the fount head of the Christian story and life spills over into the public square where it implicitly and explicitly challenges alternative stories and worldviews. The church gathers in worship as an act of defiance against earthly kingdoms and allegiance to a kingdom that is yet to come in full. The members of the church scatter to live out that kingdom life in the various corners of the world in which they live. This church—in both its gathered and scattered states—is involved in a viability contest with the stories on offer around it.

What this means is that the church—as the people of God who are tasked with living out of the gospel and engaging their roles within the story of Scripture—is to serve as an embodied apologetic. Newbigin contends the gospel must be proclaimed as the hinge of history, and it must also be lived out by a community that proves the comprehensive and holistic viability of the Bible as the one true story of the world.

If this is the church's role, it is thoroughly missionary in nature. The proclamation and embodiment of the gospel in and through individual lives takes shape and form in a community of disciples. This community exists to bring honor and praise to the God who has freely chosen to communicate his goodness to his creatures. In so doing, we find ourselves caught up into being a community that is characterized by the same concerns as those exhibited by our God: the manifestation of his goodness and the invitation to his creatures to appreciate it. The church in all of its activities, programs, and purposes exists at its core to increase the knowledge of God by making him known.

So, in answer to the "naughty question," the church exists for God's purpose to make himself known by and through his worshippers. Thus, as Newbigin argues, the church is inescapably a missionary community.

Missional Ecclesiology Applied

It has been the burden of this book to point out some of the specific issues facing the American church today and to inspect them through a missionary lens. While some of these issues are time-bound, the missionary ecclesiology of Newbigin transcends any of the particulars we have discussed and provides the church with a missional orientation to understanding itself in all times and all places.

Nonetheless, it is good to conclude our investigation with a brief glimpse toward the future of the church in light of its missionary nature. In other words, given the missionary imperative arising from the missional nature of the church, how should we respond to the types of issues we've raised? This last section, brief as it is, will offer missionary rationale for a constructive approach to the issues we've touched on. Clearly this is not comprehensive, but it aims to provide a prompt for further thought, reflection, and extended applications.

Overcoming Division through Shared Story and
Shared Mission

As we have looked at the hot-button issues addressed throughout this book, we have seen several forces of division that impose themselves upon the church from without. Newbigin, confident of the truth that Jesus's church is unified at its core around a common gospel, was helpful in pushing us to see the church should naturally express and embody a diverse unity of otherwise-different people who are connected essentially around common commitments. The very act of existing in an unexpected unity should serve as a testimony to the unifying power of the gospel to a watching world.

If we begin with this conviction and we recognize that the church is a missionary body at its core, both our nature and our purpose should push us to ensure that external forces of division are not allowed to thwart our manifestation of essential unity. This posture considers both who we are—a united community of gospel believers being discipled into living out the biblical story—and how we best display that identity to a world that is invited to join us. Our uncommon unity as a church is part of our lived-out and embodied apologetic of the truth of the gospel, and is therefore essentially connected to our missional purpose.

What these convictions will develop in us is a desire to excise any remnants of division that have entered into our fellowship from outside. This does not mean we disregard doctrinal distinctives, theological convictions, or biblical truths in pursuit of unity. It means that as we inspect our church, we are on the hunt for extra-biblical distractions that might exacerbate disunity. Two examples that we saw of occasions for this are our political allegiances and our tendency toward racial segregation.

We noted above that the false political binary that often presents itself in America comes laden with pre-existing commitments associated more with a political vision for the country than a kingdom vision for what is good. Even though many congregations may exhibit rather uniform political opinions, the church should not align with a particular party because the party is appealing to a different standard that will inevitably come into conflict with biblical standards. Rather than promoting the persuasions that are of most pressing concern and then downplaying the importance of positions that are inconsistent with biblical teaching, the church should be about the business of prophetically speaking a biblical ethic that comes before and against any particular party line.

If the church is to be missional in this area, it must do the work of living according to a different kingdom wherein Jesus is the only party whose policies are to be followed. This means that both parties will be challenged—not by the talking points of their opponents, but by the king of the universe. Such a posture demonstrates the universal biblical story that Newbigin calls the church to inhabit, and it avoids reinforcing external political divisions within the church.

Likewise, on the issue of racial segregation, we saw that the church alone has the theological resources to unite that which the world is eager to cobble together. Though it appears as an issue of acute interest in this cultural moment, unity beyond ethnic and cultural distinction has been a concern of the church since Paul confronted Peter in Galatians 2. According to Paul, on the basis of the gospel that has drawn people of diverse backgrounds into a shared family, Peter stood condemned for withdrawing table fellowship to please the circumcision party. Paul says that the gospel produces a unity that transcends any culture and any cultural moment.

While the world around us is particularly keen to discuss and address racial tensions, the church should be providing a case study for how to do it. Whereas the world sees the brokenness between ethnic groups and desires to fix it, it is only the gospel and the biblical story that provides an ontological confidence that such a unity is not only possible, but already realized in Christ. Churches, then, should not just be concerned with seeking to manifest a diverse fellowship around the gospel because it is right and good, but also because it is a missional manifestation before a watching world of the solution for a problem that is rooted in sin.

In both of these examples—and any others where potential division threatens unity—a missional ecclesiology pushes us to identify and properly address conflicts brought into the church from without. This does not mean we avoid conflict or pretend differences of culture, opinion, history, or priorities do not exist. Rather, we approach them with confidence that we are united with one another more fundamentally than we are divided from one another. We approach confrontation of such issues with the confidence that we are for one another even in the midst of difficult conversations.

Such a love-driven unity around the gospel and the shared task of helping one another to live it out is what a watching world needs to see. But to display this for the world, we need to attend to the various ways we have smuggled the idols that cause division into the sanctuary and allowed them to disrupt unity in the worship of the only one to whom worship is due.

Smashing Idols through Christocentric Worship

If idolatry is at the root of division within the church, then we find ourselves in a doubly dangerous place. First of all, offering our worship to that which is not ultimate is sinful in and of itself. Our mission as disciples is to be worshippers of God; thus, any misdirected worship is an affront to our fundamental purpose. Second, if idolatrous worship infiltrates a community of believers, then our display of the gospel is compromised. The mission of Christians and the mission of the church are compromised if there is any hint of offering worship to that which is not God.

For that reason, we have looked at ways that idolatry has crept into the church and threatened our mission. We saw this especially in the discussions of sex, individualism, and personal kingdom building that have established roots within our churches. At times, arguing that we can pursue our own kingdom and pleasure without compromising allegiance to God, we have baptized our idols rather than excising them.

If the church is a community of worshippers dedicated to living out a new way of being human in Christ, then worship of God alone must characterize our display of this new community. We know there are any number of created things that will vie for our worship—even as we enter the sanctuary. But if the sanctuary is ground-zero for displaying the redeemed community of restored worshippers in Christ, then we must be adamant about irradicating any idolatrous roots that might lie beneath the surface that would produce future idolatrous fruit.

As Newbigin reminds us, this will require us telling and retelling the one true story of the world and the God who created it. In this story neither sex nor the self, empire nor economy has any claim upon our worship. Amidst the cacophony of voices in the world that call for our allegiance, the church gathered in worship directed solely to the maker of the universe provides a contrast community. As the church refuses to worship the things the world worships, it offers the visible testimony of a more satisfying hope found in total allegiance to the God who is himself the only and ultimate good.

Rightly directed worship is more than mere avoidance of idolatry. Rightly directed worship is a missionary encounter and a confrontation of the world's systems and stories, idols and idolatries. Any issue, then, that might present itself from without should be approached from the perspective of a church tasked with worshipping God through proclaiming and manifesting what he has declared to be the proper order of things in a disordered world. Again, we glimpse the missionary nature of the church as more than a perspective or a part of the church—mission thoroughly permeates the church's essence.

Post-Inspection Living

My prayer as we conclude this investigation is that we have been able to see from a missionary's perspective some of the issues we have allowed to crowd out our missionary purpose as a church. But I also pray this inspection has started to reveal how deeply mission is at the core of God's church. If this is true, then none of the issues we have looked at, nor any other issues that might arise, will be something we can consider apart from their relation to our task of knowing God and making him known.

May it be that we would do more than merely don missionary goggles occasionally. May we see ourselves as missional people, called into churches that are missional communities, reflecting the missional heart of our God.

God's mission to make himself known is what the church is for. Our mission as God's people cannot be anything less.